I
GOT
A
NAME

I
GOT
A
NAME

The Murder of Krystal Senyk

ELIZA ROBERTSON

IN COLLABORATION WITH
MYLES DOLPHIN

HAMISH HAMILTON

an imprint of Penguin Canada, a division of Penguin Random House Canada Limited

Canada • USA • UK • Ireland • Australia • New Zealand • India • South Africa • China

First published 2023

www.penguinrandomhouse.ca

This book is non-fiction. Some names, locations, and identifying characteristics have been changed to protect the privacy of those depicted. Dialogue has been constructed from a combination of voice recordings, video footage, and memory.

LIBRARY AND ARCHIVES CANADA CATALOGUING IN PUBLICATION

Title: I got a name : the murder of Krystal Senyk / Eliza Robertson with Myles Dolphin.
Names: Robertson, Eliza, author. | Dolphin, Myles author.
Identifiers: Canadiana (print) 20210242205 | Canadiana (ebook) 20210242213 | ISBN
9780735240049
(softcover) | ISBN 9780735240056 (EPUB)
Subjects: LCSH: Senyk, Krystal. | LCSH: Bax, Ronald. | LCSH: Murder—Yukon—Carcross
Region. | LCSH:
Murder—Investigation—Yukon—Carcross Region.
Classification: LCC HV6535.C33 C37 2023 | DDC 364.152/3097191—dc23

Book and cover design by Kelly Hill
Cover images by (ladybug) © Sally Anscombe / Getty Images; (texture background)
© Alex_Po / Shutterstock.com; (Senyk house) © Whitehorse Star Collection

Printed and bound in Canada

10 9 8 7 6 5 4 3 2 1

Penguin
Random House
HAMISH HAMILTON CANADA

For Krystal
and everyone who loved her

How can a dead woman speak?

Why does she have to be dead in order to be able to speak?

And what is speech in a book of murder?

—MIEKE BAL

CONTENTS

1.

A
LINKAGE
OF
LIVES

The pages had been folded inside a No. 10 envelope and left on the porch of my childhood home. There was no return address or sender: just my name, written across the envelope in ballpoint pen. It was July 4, 2015. I was visiting home, in Victoria, for the second time since moving to England. I unfolded the contents, my eyes darting to the name at the bottom of the page. It was signed by our neighbour Lynne.

Lynne had lived up the hill for as long as I could remember. Or rather, she lived across the road and up a steep driveway. I had always felt warmly toward her and her husband, Hans, the only man on our block aside from my father to wear a beret. I didn't know the couple well, though they were part of what my dad had called, with wry affection, *the voisinage*, a rotation of neighbours who hosted unpretentious dinner parties.

I started reading Lynne's note, expecting to find an invitation or reminder—something ordinary.

I am writing to pass on a couple pages of writing from a friend of mine who was murdered in the Yukon in 1992, it began. To the extent that my attention had been open to the house around me, noting the people and ambient sounds, all my focus now funnelled to what I was reading.

Her name was Krystal Senyk.

Krystal had been best friends with a woman named Colleen[1], the letter explained. Colleen's husband, Ronald Bax, was a wilderness guide, sculptor, gun aficionado, and father to their two sons. *He was also controlling, jealous, and unstable*, the letter continued.

When Colleen decided to leave her husband, Krystal offered her and the boys her support. Ron had resented Krystal for years—he perceived her as a rival of sorts. By February 1992, his rage was getting more pointed and direct. Based on his intimidations, Krystal was starting to fear for her life. She reported his behaviour to the police, but her requests for help resulted in no action.

On the night of March 1, Krystal returned to her cabin in Carcross. Ron was waiting and shot her in the doorway to her house. When she didn't show up for work the next day, her colleagues called the police. Between Krystal's murder and the discovery of her body twelve hours later, Ronald Bax disappeared.

To this day, he has never been found.

My neighbour Lynne had worked with Krystal at the federal land claims office in Whitehorse. In the days following the murder, a colleague discovered some personal writing on Krystal's work computer. Lynne didn't know why, but the colleague printed the pages and gave them to her. That summer of 2015, while cleaning her home office, Lynne had unearthed them again.

I am handing them to you, in case you find them at all useful in your writing, she wrote in her note to me. *I know this is quite presumptuous, but your name kept popping into my head.*

There were only two pages, stapled together in the left-hand corner. At the top of the first page, Lynne had printed KRYSTAL in capital letters, underlined twice. Below her name, the years of her life: 1962–1992. Next to it, the following annotation: *Krystal Senyk murdered on March 1, 1992 by Ronald Bax in Carcross, YT.* Today, the pages are thirty years old: faintly yellowed, the text typed in 12-point Courier.

```
I am the collective gathering of all my
experiences. My behaviours and beliefs have
evolved throughout countless ages and have
currently choosen to manifest themselves
in the human form present on this earth,
in this time. You see, i am part of a con-
tinuum. A linkages of lives each unique unto
itself but forming a complete picture of the
essense of the life it was and currently is.
```

I found myself searching for an explanation—as if Krystal herself could tell me, through these words, what had happened to her. Her sentences felt instead like the opening of a well. Her voice had a rawness about it: fresh, instant, unmediated, as though composed in one chain of thought. Yet the writing was dense. At first, I found it impenetrable.

I read the pages two or three times. Then I folded the papers, very carefully, back into their envelope. I sensed that I couldn't shift my attention to Krystal's story until I could devote my whole, unbroken focus. Over the next three years, I would reread the contents of the envelope, removing the pages with equal care—less to avoid crumpling and more because I perceived in them something very dear: a call, a seed, an urgency. So dear, it immobilized me.

═══

In that time, I Googled. While the murder had attracted a local media frenzy in the 1990s, little of the case could be found online by 2015, aside from the RCMP's wanted advisory for Ronald Bax. I also discovered one or two articles that had been digitally archived: the first, published the day after Krystal's death, on the front page of the *Whitehorse Star*. "Woman Is Shot," the headline announces. "RCMP Hunt for Murder Suspect."

Online, two images sit side by side. First: Krystal at her desk, before an ordered jumble of papers and a coil notebook, pen in hand, buttoned V-neck cardigan with a scarf tucked into the collar, hair curling around her ears, mouth flat. A lightness in her gaze suggests the camera shuttered between smiles or a roll of the eyes as she waited for the photographer (a colleague, I imagine) to finish. Behind Krystal, three photos hang on the wall, maybe images she snapped herself. Two appear to be night scenes, one with a burst of luminosity I can't decipher from this distance, though it's moon-like. On the shelves, there are two potted plants and a puppet slumping against a stack of papers.

The other photo is of Ronald Bax: his eyes so resinous you can't discern his pupils. His chin is clean-shaven, but he has a blond moustache, thicker than the hair on his head, which appears thin, or thinning. I note the mole on the left side of his throat. The *Whitehorse Star* describes Bax as five feet nine inches, though the RCMP list him as five seven. I can see that he is good-looking.

In the early days of writing this book, when I Googled Krystal Senyk, the search engine returned more images of Bax. When Krystal did appear, her image was often yoked to his: a tiny injustice I would register as I took a screenshot and cropped him out of the frame.

The website I didn't stumble upon, because it didn't exist yet, would belong to former journalist Myles Dolphin: www.whathappenedtoronbax.com. On July 4, 2018, three years to the day that my neighbour introduced me to Krystal, Myles reached out to me over Instagram. He'd seen a tweet I made to a reporter who had written one of the few recent articles about the murder. The reporter had quoted from an interview with Krystal's mother, Vera Campbell. I had wanted to know if any further interviews existed. This reporter no longer worked at the *Whitehorse Star*, and the paper didn't have a forwarding address for him, but I learned that Myles had also interviewed Krystal's mother while he worked at *Yukon News* in Whitehorse. He'd had this story "to the side of his desk" since 2015, like I had. His website, which he'd launched the month before contacting me in 2018, is an impressive collage of all the research he has collected on the case, and which we would continue to gather as a team.

When Myles spoke to Krystal's mother in 2016, Krystal had been dead for twenty-four years. In that time, Vera had been updated less frequently by police. Krystal's father, Philip, had regularly checked in with the investigation, but Vera's interactions with police had been less cordial. In her own words, nothing was good enough for her back then. She was too angry. "The fight would start," she said, "and they'd argue with me, and I'd argue with them. We never got along, so they stayed away from me."

Vera and Philip had separated when Krystal was a child, and they weren't on speaking terms. When it came to the investigation, Vera was out of the loop. By the time she spoke with Myles in 2016, it had been years since the story had last been in the media. Yet she felt certain that Bax was still out there.

"After all this time, something's gotta be done. Because he's there," Vera said. "You can't just turn it aside because it's not kosher." She stressed that Myles could call her any time. "If I'm here to answer the phone, it doesn't matter. Any time, in the middle of the night, if you get a whim or a thought, you want to talk about it, you can call. I'm so happy that you're going to do something."

Maggie Nelson's book *Jane*, published in 2005, orbits the then unsolved murder of her aunt Jane in the 1960s. When Nelson wrote *Jane*, her aunt's case had remained cold for thirty-five years. Krystal's case has now been open for thirty. Most memories of her are older than I am. Perhaps every book about murder is an exercise in lateness, because our attention didn't arrive soon enough. If it had, there would be no murder, and no book—a preferable, if self-obviating, conclusion. This book and Krystal could not coexist, no more than *Jane* and Nelson's aunt Jane.

In one of the first poems, titled "Figment," Nelson's grandfather asks of her book in progress:

> *What will it be, a figment*
> *of your imagination?*[2]

In this question, he pinpoints the task, and the impossibility, of narrating a real-life story that lacks a real-life ending. How do you stitch together a person you can't talk to—who died before you were born (or in my case, when I was four)? How do you do justice to her, or to the real-life trauma that has nothing, really, to do with you? It's a funny phrase, "do justice," like we might "do laundry" or "do the ironing." The expression means to treat fairly, with full appreciation. Often it has nothing to do with justice. Except in this case, it does.

Years earlier, at the end of my undergraduate degree, I volunteered at a women's transition home in Victoria. I cleaned. I washed laundry. I sorted the clothing donations. I cared for the children when their moms needed to focus on other tasks. One day, I recognized a new resident who came in. We'd gone to high school together. It struck me then—the pervasiveness of intimate partner violence. How *ordinary* it was, if gobsmacking in its cruelty. I was trained not to acknowledge recognition when it happened. If you saw a former resident on the street, you didn't stop and ask how they were. I respected why—it preserved privacy and safety. But there was something eerie about this pretending. How everything about intimate partner violence seemed to unfold in sealed, unspeakable quiet. When she entered the living room, we held each other's gaze. She smiled uncertainly. Neither of us said a word about high school. Her daughter was two years old, and I busied myself with her care.

A decade later, I called this same transition home as I tried to support someone close to me. This person had confided in me for months, texting sometimes in the middle of the night when the abuse reached a flashpoint. I didn't know what to do. I felt scared for her and useless. Again, the silence struck me. My friend didn't want outside help, though I gave her the transition home's number just in case. Not for the first time, I found myself in an underground system of women talking to other women, or women warning other women—never in public. Rarely trusting outside authorities to intervene. How many people were in this situation, keeping the violence wilfully, resignedly quiet?

When I read my neighbour's letter in 2015, it churned something in me. Even when I had to focus on other tasks, Krystal's story roosted in the corner of my consciousness, rustling its feathers now and then, spiriting me toward two impossible missions:

1. I wanted to find Krystal Senyk.
2. I wanted to find Ronald Bax.

Even though I recognized these goals as unattainable in a material sense, they consumed me. I have tried to reach Krystal. The fragments of her preserved in photos, video, newspapers, memory—I tried to gather them, to fix them in place. I was the same age as Krystal when she died, and that coincidence meant something to me. It felt urgent to understand what had happened to her, to "make sense" of her murder. And if her murder had no "sense" to it, I wanted to demonstrate the consequences of dismissing a person's fear, of thinking this violence is private, or none of our business. I wanted to make this violence our business.

And yes, I hoped to find Ronald Bax. I could say that I desired that resolution for Krystal's family—and I do. Very much. But it has become more personal than that. For reasons I don't fully comprehend, because I don't experience them intellectually—I experience them in flushes of heat, gastric acid, and hives—I want to see Ronald Bax on trial.

In the summer of 2018, three years after I learned about Krystal's murder and a month after I began collaborating with Myles, I visited home in Victoria again. I sat with my neighbour Lynne, on her patio, which overlooks the house I grew up in. Lynne had found for me a mixtape that Krystal had given her in the early nineties. Inside the case, Krystal had hand-painted a J-card with blue and iris smudges. She'd printed the title of each track in two columns, one for each side. On the tape's adhesive label, which faced out through the plastic, she'd inscribed: *I got a name*. I later realized this was the title of the first track on the B-side, a Jim Croce song released in 1973. At that moment, however, I mistook the words for Krystal's own title for the cassette. Written in her own hand thirty years ago, it felt like a dispatch from back then—a call.

2.

SHELTER

The federal land claims office in Whitehorse sat over the Yamaha dealership at the corner of 2nd and 4th Avenues. At the top of the stairs, a counter separated reception from the doorway, with a gap at the end of the counter to pass through. In a quiet moment, you might hear the vertical blinds rasp together in the breeze from the open windows or the thump of fingers onto those bulky standard-issue keyboards. The monitors complemented the dust-rose wall trim, producing a palette as calm as any site of nineties administration. On Friday, February 28, 1992, Krystal Senyk returned to work after a week in California. She placed her hands on the counter and vaulted herself over, remarking to a colleague: "When you work at a federal land claims office, you go to Disneyland for your reality."

When I imagine this line, relayed to me by a few of her co-workers, Krystal's entrance reads like a sitcom: droll and animate, how screenwriters announce a character as larger than the rest. Realistically, she may have vaulted over the counter and continued to her cubby office, which bordered her boss's, without this aside. She might have shucked her parka and her bag and only later remarked on her holiday to colleagues, perhaps in the staff room over a communal pot of coffee. Either way, the sense presses on me: Krystal was not a woman who walked through doors. She catapulted.

Krystal grew up in the Niagara region of Ontario, where she lived for part of her childhood on a horse farm with her younger brother, Gord. She had always been physically strong—lugging buckets of warm water for the horses before she and Gord caught the school bus in the morning. After Gord's dad, Krystal's stepfather, moved out, the farm passed to their mother, Vera. Five-year-old Gord would steer the tractor, and Vera would follow on foot, hucking up bales for Krystal, eleven, to mount on the trailer. Back at the barn, they'd use augers to stack the bales up to the loft. Once, when she was around twelve, Krystal was throwing a grab hook into a bale when it sunk into her leg. Instead of crying or calling for their mother straight away, she pulled down her pants to calmly assess the wound. Like Vera, she had an independent, do-it-yourself attitude her whole life. "If there was something wrong with the truck, she'd get under there with her wrenches," Gord remembers. "Google wasn't around then. She'd ask someone how to do it and she'd go at it." That's exactly the spirit Krystal brought to her work, and everything else she set her mind to.

The Yukon is home to fourteen First Nations, whose roots extend back twelve thousand years. Yukon First Nations had rallied for autonomy since the beginning of the twentieth century, yet the federal government ignored their appeals until the 1970s. An agreement between the Council for Yukon Indians and the federal government was not ratified by the council in 1984, for several reasons, including the agreement's proposed extinguishment of Aboriginal land title (Indigenous people's inherent rights to the land), as well as its exclusion of self-government. When negotiations resumed after another year, the task for federal negotiators in Whitehorse was partly to convince their Ottawa counterparts that these talks about self-government were serious.

As an engineer, Krystal worked with her Yukon and First Nation counterparts to map each area, determining how much land each Nation would retain. Though they represented different mandates on paper, everyone on the team tended to bond. The work sometimes involved travelling to remote communities by bush plane or snowmobile, staying in rustic accommodations, and doing as much negotiation over beers as they did in the field. Most of the people who worked on these agreements resided in the Yukon. They were neighbours; they ran into each other at the same bars, baseball matches, and supermarkets. Their negotiations were principle-based rather than position-based, which meant they looked beyond resolute stances to acknowledge the basic needs, wants, and motivations of each party. From there, it would be easier to identify solutions that met everyone's goals. Or that was the idea.

In a mineral-rich territory like the Yukon, they had to consider subsurface rights as well as the land above ground. They also had to listen to the concerns of other parties, such as outfitter guides, who wanted access to the land for their businesses. Even for an engineer, the work required diplomacy, and Krystal didn't always oblige. She was someone who pursued honest, no-bullshit connection with people, but she didn't adhere to social graces just for the sake of them. My neighbour Lynne described Krystal as a "bull in a china shop," though her intentions were always heartfelt and kind.

In August 2018, I visited Whitehorse for the first time since receiving Krystal's pages. I stayed at a hostel that was so full in the summer season, they spilled accommodations onto the back lawn, where I bunked in a permanently parked Volkswagen van. Barring global pandemics, the Yukon is a hotly travelled territory, with tourists flying from all over the world to hike the Tombstone Mountains, canoe from Whitehorse to Dawson City, or watch the northern lights.

In the northernmost reaches of the territory, the sun shines 24-7 in the summer, while dark stretches all day long in the winter. It's a place of extremes: home to one of the longest rivers in Canada, for which the territory is named; roaming route for thousands of Porcupine caribou, one of the largest land migrations on the planet; site of the coldest temperature ever recorded in Canada: minus sixty-three Celsius, on February 3, 1947, in a ghost town called Snag. (As a point of comparison, the average temperature on Mars is minus sixty.) There's a sense of separation between the Yukon and the southern provinces, which has been encoded in local turns of speech. It's common for residents to refer to every place outside the territory as simply "outside": *So-and-so's outside at the moment.* The first time I heard this expression, I thought they'd stepped out for a cigarette. But no: they'd driven down to BC.

This wasn't my first trip here. In 2013, after my father's death, my mom, brother, and I piled into our family Mazda and drove 3500 kilometres north. I had set a novel in Dawson City, so it was a research visit of sorts, though it was also a manic displacement of our grief, a way to try on this new unit of three. We would continue up the Dempster Highway all the way to Inuvik, above the Arctic Circle, but we spent a night in Whitehorse, where we visited a family friend. Later, I would learn that this friend had also known Krystal Senyk. She and her husband had a cabin on Crag Lake, where Krystal had lived. One summer, they helped Krystal reshingle her roof. Krystal was friendly with their young children. She had even given them their first pets, twin kittens.

Five years after that visit, I returned to the Yukon. I sat with our family friend in her home, and we talked about Krystal.

In the weeks leading up to the murder, Krystal had been feeling more and more distressed, our family friend told me—breaking into tears whenever she tried to confide what was going on. "This was Krystal?" our friend later wrote to Krystal's father,

Philip, in Ontario. Even through Krystal's kidney problems, which had sent her to a hospital in BC the year before, this friend had never seen her so scared or disarmed.

"What was Ron doing?" I asked.

"He was acting very creepy toward her. If they were in a store at the same time, he would gaze at her with hate."

After the murder, she had wanted it on record that she had concerns about how the RCMP handled the case. She went down to the police station herself and reminded them that Krystal had asked for help several times and that they'd dismissed her fear as an overreaction. One officer had advised Krystal: "If he does come around, invite him in for tea and talk to him. That will calm him down."

Later, Myles and I would read an RCMP warrant to search the business premises of NorthwesTel. The officer who requested the warrant, an active investigator on Krystal's case, sought the subscriber information and long-distance tolls between two telephone numbers, one linked to Carcross, the other to Whitehorse. The officer suspected that one number was issued to Ronald Bax, the second to Krystal Senyk. The records he requested extend from January 1992—right after Ron and Colleen separated on December 26—to March 1992, when Krystal was murdered, which suggests he was investigating whether Ron had been terrorizing Krystal by phone. Whatever his tactics, everyone who knew Krystal at that time reported the same thing: she feared for her life.

Our family friend's husband had worked as a counsellor. He had professional experience in spousal violence. After he and Krystal spoke, he agreed she was vulnerable: when Colleen sought refuge in the transition home, Ron might hit a flashpoint of rage, and Krystal could become the target. In that letter to Krystal's dad composed after the murder, our friend would write: *In a situation where power and control are the drivers, the target is whoever thwarts it.*

The counsellor referred Krystal to the transition home in Whitehorse where Colleen herself would be moving. He advised she avoid time alone, so Krystal stayed above a friend's store in Whitehorse for two weeks. She planned to fly to California at the end of February, when Colleen would be delivering custody papers to Ronald Bax. He would be furious, Krystal knew. Ron blamed her for the separation, even if she had nothing to do with it, even if the marriage was collapsing long before Krystal arrived in the Yukon. She needed to get out of town.

As we finished our chat that day, our family friend left me with a few photocopies: the letter to Krystal's dad, which she never brought herself to send; two pages of the transition home logbook, which recorded check-ins and departures on the last day of Krystal's life; and a forty-page report written by a lawyer on behalf of the transition home. The report was addressed to one of the founders of LEAF, the Women's Legal Education and Action Fund. Little did I know at the time, Philip Senyk would spend years trying to obtain this report. The lawyer had interviewed three staff members in the days following Krystal's murder. From their memories, the last night of Krystal's life is patched together.

"I will warn you that the report makes for painful reading," the lawyer wrote in the letter that prefaces the report. "So, find a comfortable spot, get a cup of coffee, and get prepared to be very angry and sorrowful."

I was at the Midnight Sun coffee shop, close to our family friend's house, when I absorbed these words. I sat at a quiet table, as far as I could from the counter, and read. My knuckles whitened around the ballpoint pen in my hand, which I clutched as a fidget tool more than anything. Occasionally I underlined a sentence, scribbled a question, or scrawled in the margins: *?!*

"It is my profound hope that these facts will be of use in making some specific changes in the way our institutions respond to the horrific cruelty faced by women and children," the lawyer writes.

> This is the sixth death that I am personally aware of in the Yukon where a woman has died at the hands of an angry man. In each case, the police knew or ought to have known the danger the women faced and failed to protect her. I have seen no systemic changes whatever that bear the scars or the lessons of those deaths. It is my intent that this one will be different. We must use the most difficult truths to demand the most effective change.

Colleen first visited the transition home on February 18, 1992, to see if it would be an appropriate option for her and her sons. She told the staff member that she had been separated from Ron for several weeks but he was still playing mind games with her. He would drive to where she was staying with friends and sit outside for hours, even when it was freezing outside. One of those friends had a baby, and Colleen was getting nervous for their safety. Her lawyer was about to deliver custody papers to Ron's lawyer, which would enrage him. She needed a safe place to stay until the worst blew over.

Krystal called the transition home the next day, expressing her concern that when Colleen went into the shelter, she herself would become Ron's target. Krystal was physically strong, and a champion arm wrestler, but Ron made a point of telling Colleen he could "take Krystal out." He had banned her from the house for the past two years and wouldn't let their boys visit her, though she was close with them, like an aunt.

Colleen stayed at the transition home for a week, while Krystal went to Disneyland. In that time, Colleen left numerous messages with her lawyer. She needed a restraining order before moving out of the transition home on the twenty-ninth, and as that day approached, her messages became more and more urgent. The lawyer never returned her calls.

Krystal picked Colleen and the boys up on the morning of February 29 to help them move into a new rental property, where she would spend the night to help them get settled. The next day, March 1, Ron showed up at the new house while they were unpacking. He demanded to take the kids to an air show that afternoon. He was supposed to organize visits through their mutual friend Suzanne—she was close with all three of them, Colleen, Krystal, and Ron—but he often ignored this arrangement. There wasn't yet a custody agreement in place, which is why Colleen had hired a lawyer. After some debate, she let the boys go with him.

Though the air show was supposed to last from noon to three, Ron returned forty-five minutes later—the first sign something was wrong. He stood outside the house with their three-year-old in his arms, their five-year-old standing beside him. The younger boy said he wanted to stay with their dad, which Colleen attributed to Ron's manipulation. (He had previously taught their son to say some abusive phrases. One of them was "Krystal's a fuck.") Ron said that if she didn't let him see the kids, she wouldn't be seeing them either—or himself. Colleen and Ron began to argue, and for the first time, Colleen felt she stood up for herself. She told him he had no right to be on her property and she demanded that he leave. Ron was holding their youngest while this argument unfolded.

Colleen asked him whether he'd received the letter from her lawyer yet, the one that proposed she gain custody. Ron said he hadn't seen the letter, that he didn't have a lawyer anymore, and that she wouldn't need one either. She asked what he meant by that. He told her to figure it out. This comment scared Colleen; she interpreted it as a death threat to herself. The argument took place outside the house.

When he saw Krystal inside, he flipped his middle finger at her.

Sometime later, Krystal was buttoning her parka to leave when the phone rang. It was Suzanne, saying she was extremely worried for their safety because Ron had just phoned. He'd told Suzanne to tell Colleen that "the hunt is on." He continued: "The hunt begins tomorrow. Oh, forget it. I'm on my way." Then he hung up. Colleen wrote these words down on a Kleenex, the nearest paper at hand.

Suzanne was so concerned that she had already called the police. Ron hunted big game for a living. He had every capacity to make good on his threats.

Krystal drove Colleen and her sons back to the transition home. The boys were agitated, confused about returning to the shelter so soon. They'd only left the day before. They wanted to go home. Krystal fried cheese sandwiches for them in the kitchen while Colleen waited for the RCMP in the smoking room.

Colleen paced the smoking room, which adjoined the front porch, surrounded by windows. A staff member waited with her. Colleen's distress unsettled her too. She hadn't thought about it before, the vulnerability of all this glass on the ground floor. Colleen showed the staff member the tissue, where she had written Ron's message.

"What does he mean by hunt?" the staff member asked.

Colleen explained that he hunted, that he owned a number of guns.

When the RCMP officer arrived, Colleen told him about the altercation that afternoon and about Ron's threat that she wouldn't see him or the children anymore. Ron had threatened suicide before, to keep her from leaving, but now he was extending this threat to their kids. She showed the officer the words she'd scrawled on the tissue and explained how dangerous Ron was.

The officer said the police couldn't get involved in domestic disputes until someone broke the law, such as by violating a restraining order. Colleen said she'd been trying to get a restraining order all week but that her lawyer hadn't returned her calls.

The officer replied, "Well, we can talk to him until we're blue in the face, but it probably won't do any good." The best thing for Colleen, he repeated, was to obtain a restraining order.

But Ron didn't fear courts or lawyers. That he had "no respect for the law" was even written on Colleen's transition home intake form. He wouldn't stay away from her or the kids just because a court told him to.

"When my lawyer serves the custody papers, he'll flip," she told the officer. "This guy is out to kill himself or one of us."

The transition home staff member agreed that Colleen should be afraid for her safety. Ron was exhibiting enraged, erratic behaviour, and he had the weapons to make good on his threats.

Once more, the officer recited his advice: go see your lawyer, get a restraining order. He said Colleen had done the right thing by coming to the transition home. This was the right space for her. The officer said he could drive around and look for Ron, but talking didn't do much good in these cases. They couldn't arrest Ron or bring him in until he broke the law.

Colleen said she'd try to obtain the restraining order first thing in the morning, even if she had to camp in her lawyer's office. She feared Ron would show up at her workplace, a daycare. She knew she couldn't go to work until she got the order, no matter how long it took.

When it was Krystal's turn to speak with the officer, she told him that Ron blamed her for the breakup of his marriage. Like Colleen, Krystal's eyes flickered to the window as she spoke. She wanted to go home that night. She hadn't returned yet after her weeks away, because she'd been helping Colleen move. She'd borrowed a truck from a friend, and she was supposed to return it that night. She also needed to keep the stove lit so her pipes didn't freeze, or her animals. She had three dogs and several cats. She'd been away from them for a long time now. But Ron hated her. Now that Colleen was safe, she said, she worried he would target her. She asked if the police could check her place before she went home.

The officer asked where she lived. She told him it was seven miles on the other side of Ron and Colleen's place on Tagish Road. That was an hour outside of Whitehorse, so she suggested the officer call the cops in Carcross. She gave him two names and asked him to phone the detachment.

He replied that both of those officers were "doing their own thing" that night. One was away at a conference and the other was visiting friends. Neither would be at the station.

Krystal asked if he could lay charges against Ron for the threats he'd made. The officer repeated that he couldn't do anything unless Ron broke the law. He recommended she get her own lawyer and go through the court system.

"Forget it," Krystal said. She couldn't afford a lawyer. She thought she'd try to get included in Colleen's restraining order.

"Could you at least look for him?" she tried again.

The officer said they could cruise around and look for him, but it might not do any good.

"Could you do that before I go home to Carcross?"

The officer said he couldn't promise they would find him that night. He suggested she stay at a friend's.

When she asked whether police from Whitehorse could follow her home to make sure she got there safely, he said no, that wasn't their job.

"What am I supposed to do?" she asked. "This guy drives 140 kilometres an hour. If he sees me, he'll run me off the road."

The officer suggested her request for an escort was unreasonable and not a good use of their time.

"I know he's out to get me," Krystal said.

At this point the transition home staff member interjected. She explained that Ron had dropped his lawyer. Colleen would have to go through him directly to negotiate custody and access to the children. The kids were important to Ron, she pointed out. What if he tried to take them?

The officer said, "No judge on God's green earth would allow kids to be separated from their mother."

The staff member asked whether there was any kind of protection Krystal could access. Once more, he offered to drive around and look for Ron, but again said that it wouldn't do any good to talk to him, which is all they could do at this point.

Krystal asked the officer if he knew what vehicle Ron was driving.

The officer pulled a piece of paper from his pocket and read off a description of a brown truck.

"No," she said, disturbed that the cop didn't even know what vehicle he was looking for. "He's driving a blue Ford Tempo." The brown truck was sitting at home in Carcross.

The officer wrote *blue Ford Tempo* on a piece of paper and placed it in his pocket. The entire evening, that was the only note he wrote down.

After her conversation with the officer, Krystal returned to the dining room. "What needs to happen around here?" she asked the staff member waiting for her. "Does there need to be a body before they take this seriously?"

"Unfortunately," the staff member said, "that seems to be the way it goes." Her own sister had been murdered by her ex-husband. She told Krystal she understood the seriousness of the situation, that Ron's threats should not be underestimated. She talked about the cycle of violence, how the dynamics of abuse worsen over time.

Krystal was nodding and repeating, "Yes!," as if she knew all this and she was relieved to speak with someone who understood.

She asked if she could make some toast or have a bowl of

cereal—she hadn't eaten all day. The staff member told her to help herself.

While she was eating, she looked at the staff member and said, very genuinely, "Thank you."

She told the staff member about her cabin, how she was renovating it herself. She was anxious to get back. She didn't like spending much time in town.

Later, Krystal called her friend to say she would return his truck the next morning. Then she poked her head in the office to say goodnight.

"You're not going home, are you?" the staff member asked.

Krystal said she'd stay with her friend Suzanne that night.

"Are you sure you're comfortable leaving here?"

They had already offered her a bed for the night, but she'd declined. "It's okay. I'll be fine."

On her way out, she asked Colleen, "Do you think he has guns on him?"

"Yeah," Colleen answered. "He always has guns on him."

Suzanne went ice skating with her son that evening, and when they returned from the rink, Krystal was already at their house.[1] She had wanted to speak with Suzanne's husband. Graham was a friend of Ron's—they had once collaborated on a mobile for Yukon College, a flock of snowbirds. Ron had sculpted the birds, while Graham constructed the hardware to hang them over the stairs. Krystal considered Graham to be a level-headed person, and she wanted to get his sense of things.

Ron's threats were unfathomable to Graham. He was in a bad place, clearly, but there's no way he'd follow through on his words.

Suzanne wasn't so sure. Her husband had never seen Ron's violent side—which Suzanne had, a couple weeks back, when she went with Colleen to pick up her belongings. Nor had Graham heard the desperation in Ron's voice on the phone.

Suzanne tried to persuade Krystal to stay that night. They had a sofa bed. They could talk it over in the morning.

Krystal refused. "Graham doesn't think Ron will do anything drastic," she said.

She'd been away for almost three weeks at this point—only to avoid her best friend's husband. Her home meant everything to her; she'd constructed much of it herself. She wanted to return to it.

When she left Suzanne's that evening, her final words were: "I'm tired of living my life according to Ron."

The next morning, Suzanne tried calling Krystal at home before she would have left for work. She wanted to make sure she'd gotten home okay. There was no answer. She decided to wait until she arrived at the land claims office; the drive would take forty-five minutes or so. When it was time, she phoned there. The receptionist told her that Krystal hadn't arrived yet. Fifteen minutes later, she still hadn't shown up. Suzanne's stomach started to knot.

"How often is she late for work?" she asked.

"Never," said the receptionist.

She kept trying Krystal's house, but no one answered.

Finally, she called the RCMP and identified herself as the woman who had phoned the night before. She said she couldn't get hold of Krystal, that she hadn't shown up for work. Could they send someone to check on her?

The police said that unfortunately, their two guys in Carcross were busy with something on Skagway road, also known as the South Klondike Highway. They didn't have any personnel to check on Krystal. They suggested Suzanne check on her friend herself if she was so worried.

She considered that strange advice, but eventually concluded, yes, Krystal was her friend, why didn't she go check. She called her husband at work to tell him what was going on, that she was going to drive down to Carcross. He didn't think it was a good idea and asked her to wait. But she couldn't just sit there—she was too anxious—so she climbed into her car anyway. Except her engine wouldn't start. Suzanne was stranded at home in spite of herself, buzzing with nerves.

The police called back an hour later. "Is there anybody with you?"

"No . . ."

"Is there a neighbour you can go to?"

She didn't have neighbours—she lived next to a storefront. She didn't really know the people who ran it.

"Leave your house now and stay with the neighbours. We'll pick you up there."

She waited outside the building until an unmarked Blazer appeared. They drove to the Carcross cut-off, the intersection of the South Klondike Highway and the Alaska Highway twenty minutes outside Whitehorse. Suzanne sat with a detective, who asked her to scan oncoming cars—did anyone look like Ron, or did she see one of his vehicles? Eventually, an RCMP cruiser came to get her, and they drove to the school to collect her son.

While this unfolded, Colleen and an advocate from the transition home went straight to her lawyer's office to insist on getting the restraining order. After some negotiation with the lawyer, who first questioned how necessary the restraining order was, since Ron's lawyer didn't consider him dangerous, they scheduled a court appearance for later that day.

After that, they went to the RCMP station, as, according to Colleen's advocate, what the officer had told Colleen the night before about not being able to lay charges was "bullshit." At the station, the advocate informed the receptionist that they had come to press charges against Ronald Bax for uttering threats and possibly assault. She said there should be a file open, as at least two people had reported the threats to the police and the police had interviewed Colleen and Krystal at the transition home the night before.

The receptionist couldn't find any file. Colleen spelled the names of the people it could be listed under: Colleen, Ron Bax, Krystal Senyk, or Suzanne, who had called in the previous night (and again in the morning). There were no files under any of those names.

They soon met with an officer, who said, "I know this is hard for you, but you'll have to wait out here for a while." Neither Colleen nor her advocate knew what he was talking about. The advocate told him why they were there.

Hearing about the threats and possible assault, the officer took them into a back office. They discussed the dynamics of Ron's abuse, which the officer empathized with. They expressed their frustration about the police refusing to lay charges. The interview took two hours, during which time the officer kept leaving the room and coming back with more questions. Slowly, it grew clear to Colleen and the advocate that he knew more about the case than either of them did.

Colleen told the officer that recently Ron had been speaking of suicide and said he would get back at her by leaving notes for the kids that said Mommy had killed him. She had been so concerned, she'd contacted Ron's brother in Ontario and asked him to come for a visit. He stayed for a week, though Ron let them speak for only thirty minutes, at a restaurant in Whitehorse.

The brother told Colleen that he had read a book, and Ron was just going through what many men go through when their wives leave them. He said the best thing would be for Colleen to leave the kids with Ron and go on holiday. At the end of the meeting, Ron appeared in the window, folded his hand like a gun, and pointed it at Colleen.

Colleen told the police how Ron stalked her. He would sit in the car outside whatever house she was visiting, when she was with friends, even when it was below zero. He had pushed and dragged her in and out of cars. He made it clear that no one would tell him when he could see his kids.

The officer ordered lunch for Colleen and her advocate, which confirmed to the advocate that something serious was going on. The police station had never treated her or a woman from the home so well. Typically they experienced the opposite.

Over the next while, the officer continued to periodically come back into the room. He asked Colleen to draw a diagram of their house in Carcross, the yard and entrances to it off Tagish Road. At one point, the advocate overheard phrases like "ten men" and "get the police dog out."

They hadn't planned to mention the restraining order, because in the advocate's experience, the police would consider the matter taken care of and not proceed with laying charges. However, it was close to their court appointment, and they had to return to the lawyer's office.

The officer told them he didn't want either of them to leave the police station, and that the advocate should call the lawyer and tell her that.

Eventually, another staff member from the transition home arrived with Colleen's boys. She asked Colleen if she knew why she was being kept at the station.

She was there to press charges, Colleen said, for Ron's threats.

The staff member realized no one had told them. "There's been a murder," she said.

A terrible moment passed.

"Krystal?" Colleen said.

"Yeah." It wasn't confirmed, but they knew it was Ron who did it.

"She was supposed to stay at Suzanne's," Colleen said. She started talking about her children. The staff member tried to redirect the conversation back to the murder. Colleen told her she couldn't talk about it. She couldn't handle it right now. She switched the conversation back to the children.

Eventually, the police led Colleen downstairs. Suzanne was waiting for her.

Colleen still couldn't believe what everyone was telling her. "The father of my boys would not kill Krystal," she said. "The father of my boys would not kill Krystal."

Several hours passed before the Emergency Response Team arrived from BC. The Yukon didn't have their own at that time. They tear-gassed Ron's home in Carcross and searched his property. He wasn't there.

Later, they took Colleen back to the house so she might identify what items were missing. By the time they were finished, tear gas powder coated Colleen's hair, her jeans. It was wedged in her eyes. The chemicals glued to everything in the house; she couldn't get the smell out.

After reading the lawyer's report, written on behalf of the transition home, I sat in a stunned silence. The story felt familiar: the trope of someone asking for help and not being listened to. To be so afraid for your life, and to have your fear discarded. I was incensed at the constable who had gone to the transition home. His fumbling returns to Colleen's sanctity as a mother ("no judge on God's green earth . . ."), while dismissing her fear at the same time. How he stumped back to this flimsy assumption that Ron would leave them alone once Colleen had a restraining order—as if a restraining order was easy or efficient to obtain in the first place. And I felt special rancour for the lawyer who failed to communicate with Colleen all week, because who knows, that *might* have made a difference.

Even at the time, I recognized my logic as desperate, for it presupposed the police didn't already have good reason to arrest Ronald Bax. And they did.

In her covering letter to this report, the lawyer cites section 261.1 (1) of the Criminal Code, which makes it an offence to utter threats of bodily harm. She references another case in the Yukon where a woman tried to get a peace bond after her husband flew into her remote mining camp and threatened to kill her. Then, too, the police said they could do nothing. The husband returned a few months later and murdered the woman and her sister.

"They do not use these sections of the Code in patently appropriate circumstances," the lawyer writes. "Women are dying as a result." She adds that the justice system needs to confront this "cavalier police arrogance and ignorance."

It would appear that at least three people reported Ron Bax's threats in the weeks preceding Krystal's murder, and no one took notes or recorded the calls. Not the constable who went to the transition home. No one at the police station in Whitehorse. No one at the police station in Carcross. Later, I would pick apart my anger—I even felt ashamed, because it seemed to expose my naiveté (that police always come when they are called, and that when they arrive, they help). But in that moment, confronting this simple equation of someone's fear repeatedly, systemically denied: I was furious.

3.

EVERYWHERE
WHERE
THERE
IS
WATCHING

The day after we read the report, Myles drove us to Krystal's former land in Carcross. To reach Carcross from Whitehorse, you head down the South Klondike Highway past Emerald Lake—a basin exquisitely turquoise from sun reflecting off the white marl—and Carcross Desert, a single square mile of sand dunes. Krystal's lot has since been sold back to Carcross/Tagish First Nation, and the house is no longer standing. The only clue to its location is a highway marker that identifies the spot as Historic Mile 7 of Tagish Road, which was mentioned in one of the early newspaper articles.

The cabin had stood at Porcupine Creek, which threads from Caribou Mountain toward the western end of Crag Lake, thirteen minutes from Carcross and about an hour out of Whitehorse. If you were standing on Krystal's property back then, facing her cabin, Nares Mountain would loom before you, Caribou Mountain at your back. Today, all that remains is a large pit with a few severed pipes and foundations, patches of gravel, wood stakes impaled in earth, dry sedges, fireweed, bird bones, a panorama of low hills and mountains that cup the land like a stupendously painted bowl. Hidden in the trees behind the property, easily missed, Krystal's outhouse remains: a homely log structure with a tin roof and blue foam toilet seat, a crescent moon carved in the door. The outhouse is stuffed with children's toys, including a Tonka fire engine and a blue stegosaurus. Another family may have lived on the property before it was torn down, but it seems possible these toys belonged to Colleen's sons, who spent time at Krystal's cabin.

Later, Myles dropped me back at the hostel in Whitehorse. I was restless and decided to walk to the store for groceries. Maybe thirty seconds from the hostel, on the same street, I saw the sign for the transition home where Krystal and Colleen had sought help on the last night of Krystal's life. Whitehorse is not a large town, but I had no idea I'd booked accommodation so close. As I noted this, a fox sauntered across the street several feet from me. Not a runty animal, like some of the foxes you see in England, but full-bodied, as if pelted for winter, in a coat of carroty red. I proceeded to see foxes for the next three days, two or three different ones, which the hostel owner raised an eyebrow at. They're in the area, she said, but normally they avoid people. We realized—when I stepped in a fresh offering of poo three mornings in a row, after nights she'd kept her dog inside— that the foxes had been eliminating outside my VW van's door.

Red animals had been on my radar that summer. Six weeks earlier, one of my close friends, Jasmine, was visiting from Houston, Texas. She was with me when Myles got in touch in early July. Around this time, I had a few friends over, and Krystal's story came up. With Jasmine's prodding, I retrieved her written pages from my files. I hadn't opened them in months, though her story never strayed far from my mind. I began reading her words aloud—the only time I did so in front of other people and probably the last time

I will. Though it sounds sensational to say so, something shifted in the room. No one spoke for a while. We each scanned the space around us, as if searching for whatever had entered. Eventually, Jasmine broke the silence. She noticed, above my head, a red moth.

The moth flickered to the wall above my fridge, which is where I last saw it. It disappeared after that night. I've never seen one in my apartment again. A few days later, Myles and I spoke on the phone for the first time. I was thinking of Krystal so fixedly that I wondered if the moth would return. As I listened to Myles, I wandered over to the fridge and looked at the wall above it, to check. In the same square inch where I'd last seen the moth, a lady-bug perched. I smiled, allowing myself to interpret these visitors as omens. The messenger had shape-shifted, retaining only her colour, but I felt pleased, even relieved, to see her. I hesitate to share the following detail, in case it sounds embellished, but at the next moment, the door handle turned. I glimpsed the motion from the corner of my eye, then pivoted to watch it. I didn't say anything to Myles, who was still on the phone with me. A neighbour must have tried the wrong apartment by accident, I reasoned. When I opened the door, the hall was empty. I hadn't heard footsteps. But I suppose I could have missed them.

Maggie Nelson describes her mental state as she wrote *Jane: A Murder* in her later book, *The Red Parts*:

> I began to suffer from an affliction I came to call "murder mind." I could work all day on my project with a certain distance, blithely looking up "bullet" or "skull" in my rhyming dictionary. But in bed at night I found a smattering of sickening images of violent acts ready and waiting for me. Reprisals of the violence done unto Jane, unto

the other Michigan Murder girls, unto my loved ones, unto myself, and sometimes, most horridly, done by me. These images coursed through my mind at random intervals, but always with the slapping, prehensile force of the return of the repressed.[1]

She wrote of her aunt's murder from the bottom floor of a nineteenth-century house in Connecticut. Nelson describes the nights she couldn't sleep, pacing her apartment's so-called "Ponderosa Room" in a pale bathrobe, whiskey in hand. "I began to feel like a ghost," she divulges. "A stranger to myself."

She admits that she never thought "her Jane" would approximate the "real Jane." She never "had designs on such a thing": "But whoever 'my Jane' was, she had certainly been alive with me, for me, for some time."[2]

I resonate with this last sentiment strongly. I never met Krystal. I can only hope the version of her I recover in this book might approximate, in a fractional sense, the real Krystal who lived. But whoever "my Krystal" is, she has been alive with me for some time. My own version of murder mind has been less defined by ghastly images and more an urge to meet Krystal in real life. To befriend her. Often, as I interviewed Krystal's friends and family, I caught myself thinking: "I can't wait to meet her."

In *Specters of Marx*, Derrida describes ghosts as existing neither inside nor outside the head. He translates the German phrase *es spukt* ("is haunted") as a sort of ghostly return: "a stranger who is already found within."[3] The red animals represented this for me: a presence when I searched for one. The scholar or seeker should learn how to talk with the ghost, writes Derrida, "how to let thus speak or how to give them back speech . . . They are always *there,* specters, even if they do not exist, even if they are no longer, even if they are not yet."[4]

This sentiment is soothing to me: that someone who is "no longer" also resides in the hopeful, future "not yet."

Not long after my week in Whitehorse, in 2018, I flew to London for the first time since I'd moved back to Canada the year prior. I was thinking of Krystal daily at this stage: talking with her, inviting her into my mind, trying to leave room for her to speak to me, even if she was no longer, or not yet. One night as I walked alone back to where I was staying, I passed a yellow real estate sign with the boldface company name Krystal. Not five minutes later, as I passed a city park, I heard a rustling on the other side of a fence. A fox, on inspection. This one seemed even more misplaced—this was central London, after all, although urban foxes are becoming more populous there. I would continue to see foxes for the next three months, the next one at a writing residency in Switzerland.

Carl Jung describes synchronicity as a meaningful coincidence, or acausal connection, with a certain numinous quality. He relates a story where a client of his shared a dream about a golden scarab at a pivotal moment in their session. While Jung listened, he heard a tapping at his window. He opened the glass and an insect flew in: the nearest simulacrum of a gold scarab one finds in northern latitudes, a scarabaeid beetle with yellow wing cases called a rose chafer.

"There is one common flow," Jung quotes the Greek physician Hippocrates, "one common breathing, all things are in sympathy."[5] This idea would return to me as I spotted more foxes, both live and taxidermied; as I returned from Whitehorse to find a gift from a friend who knew nothing of my project—a red moth mounted inside a glass frame; as I continued to see ladybugs—in Montreal, in February, when it was minus twenty outside, or in summer, landing on my bare arm as I walked down the road.

Jung also quotes the ancient Chinese philosopher Lao-Tzu:

We put thirty spokes together and call it a wheel; but it is
on the space where there is nothing that the utility of the
wheel depends. We turn clay to make a vessel; but it is
on the space where there is nothing that the utility of the
vessel depends. We pierce doors and windows to make
a house; and it is on these spaces where there is nothing
that the utility of the house depends. Therefore just as we
take advantage of what is, we should recognize the utility
of what is not.[6]

For many, the concept of synchronicity will amount to nothing, but it has been my practice to recognize the utility of what is
not. Especially in this story, where Krystal is dead, and Bax has
vanished. Two principal players are, indeed, naught. I study the
edges: memories of Krystal, memorabilia, accounts of what happened the night of her murder, the systemic failure to protect her,
all that has transpired since. But I feel tugged equally to the gaps:
the spaces between the spokes.

In the early stages of writing this book, I transcribed Krystal's pages
for the first time—re-enacting her keystrokes, mapping the same
paths with my hands, like tracing boot prints in snow. I'd barely
transcribed a paragraph before I heard a crash of water, which split
through my noise-cancelling headphones. It sounded as though
someone had turned on my shower, but I live alone, and the taps
were off. No appliances were running. I followed the sound downstairs, edging down the steps, when I saw it: water cascading from
my ceiling. To this day, I don't understand why, or where it came

from. No appliances sit above this part of my wall, no pipes to my knowledge. But my downstairs floor was soaked.

"Only mortals can watch over [the dead], and can watch, period," writes Derrida. But "ghosts can do so as well," he continues. "They are everywhere where there is watching."[7]

Krystal's good friend and colleague Kim Hudson recalls a time when Krystal grew fascinated with the idea of past and future lives. One day, on the fall equinox, Krystal climbed a mountain on her own, either Caribou or Nares in Carcross. She wanted to clear her mind and simply be open—to a visitor, a greeting, a sign. She waited all day, from sunrise to sunset. "I'll be there," she told Kim—for whatever or whoever might come.

This story helped me understand Krystal's own words, in the pages my neighbour passed on to me.

```
The request comes from a voice soothingly
familiar to my core but unknown from my
acquaintances on this earth. With resonate
determination i search, absorbed within
my line, until this face becomes a sea of
darkness and my world centres on the depth
perception of lives once lived but now frag-
mented in memory recall. Intently, i stand
looking for a glimmer of recognition and
periodically it is mine.
```

Since hearing Kim's story, I've wanted to climb my own mountain and linger, as Krystal did, in this parallel glitch of time. I imagine us in split-screen, on our respective rocks and states of waiting.

4.

THE
SENYKS

The first time I called Paul Senyk, I did so by accident. It was the summer of 2018, weeks before I flew to the Yukon. I was trying to reach Krystal's father, Philip. Myles had passed along two numbers from Canada411, both for "P. Senyk." He hadn't tried either of them yet. The first was out of service. I dialed the second.

When someone answered, my stomach clenched. I hated cold-calling people. I rarely phoned my friends and family without pre-arranging it, never mind calling a stranger—never mind to inquire about their deceased daughter.

"Hi," I said. "Am I speaking to Philip Senyk?"

"No," he said. "This is his brother, Paul."

I introduced myself and asked if he could spare a few moments. He didn't sound enthusiastic, but suggested now was as good a time as any.

I told him that my childhood neighbour had worked with Krystal in Whitehorse, that she had given me a few pages Krystal had written on her work computer. "I'm a writer," I explained. "I'd like to write a book about your niece."

I braced for him to hang up or tell me to get lost, but to my surprise, his tone softened. He said it was nice of me to take an interest.

Paul described his niece as "a beautiful, bubbly girl. She was friends with everyone. Very smart. Well educated." He said that Krystal's father lived nearby in Niagara, but he was in a home with dementia. Any mention of Krystal was emotionally triggering for him.

Paul's tone sharpened as he discussed the police. He said they "lied like hell down there." "They told me they shot out Bax's house," he said—referring to the period when RCMP waited outside Bax's residence until the Emergency Response Team arrived.

When Paul and Philip went to Whitehorse for the funeral, they drove by Bax's house themselves. They saw no bullet holes. They confronted police on this point, and an officer allegedly replied, "Well, we didn't think you would check."

Our conversation turned to the night of Krystal's murder.

"They said it was too far to drive her back," Paul said, a note of scorn in his voice.

He'd recently been in contact with Suzanne, the last person who saw Krystal alive. He'd try to find her phone number, he offered. She lived in North Bay.

He still had some of Krystal's things in a trailer—Philip had kept them there for safekeeping. I could come by and look through them, but not for a few weeks. He was about to leave town for his cottage.

To think about a person for three years—to comb the internet for crumbs of her existence—to cohabit with these crumbs in my imagination until they felt like a real person, even a friend—and for her uncle to tell me they'd kept a trailer of her things—let's say I struggled to keep my tone even.

"Oh!" I said. "That would be incredible. Thank you. I'll call back next month. Do you have any questions for me? About our plans, or anything at all?"

He couldn't think of any. I gave him my phone number just in case.

In the end, that would be our last real phone conversation. I called several more times that summer, but either he didn't answer, or he said his basement was flooding, or he was on his way back to the family cottage. He never sounded disturbed to hear from me; indeed his tone remained warm and convivial. Every few weeks, I would try again, but eventually, he stopped answering.

I worried their family no longer supported this book, or that something had happened to Paul. He was in his eighties when we first spoke, and I had no clue how he was doing. In the end, Myles and I tracked down Paul's son Jay on Facebook. I sent Jay a message in March 2019, explaining who I was, my previous conversations with Paul, and asked if his dad's contact information had changed.

Jay replied three days later:

Hello, yes Krystal was my very close cousin. I have talked to her father and my father Paul and we decided not to be involved and do not wish to take part in this. It's a very hard subject for Krystal's dad and he does not want to revisit that part of his life. I'm sorry we could not be more help to you. Take care and best wishes.

I was crestfallen. Paul's encouragement had bolstered my confidence to pursue this story. It didn't feel right to continue without the family's support. And what was in those boxes? What if they contained diaries or letters? More than anything, I wanted Krystal to speak for herself.

Jay added a second message, immediately after the first:

Due to an illness, it's hard for her father to bring things up from the past and he has a hard time remembering things on a daily basis. I'm very sorry about this. I'm touched that you want to write about Krystal. It was very hard for me. She lived with us for years, she was like a big sister to me.

I told Jay that I respected his family's position. I said the door would remain open if anyone changed their mind. I added that Myles and I would share any information that surfaced from our research if they wanted—that we were pursuing a few unresolved tips.

Jay messaged again, mentioning a tip he'd heard from his uncle Philip, about a call from a sex worker in Michigan, where Bax's sister lived at the time. The sex worker had told police that she'd had a client who matched Bax's description. I expressed my surprise—I knew one of Bax's siblings had lived in Michigan, but I hadn't heard about the call from the sex worker. Jay sent another message after, detailing the tattoos this man had, according to the woman who called.

I was puzzled. On the one hand, Jay made it clear that his family didn't wish to contribute to our research. On the other, I got the sense he wanted to talk. In his next message, he mentioned an anecdote I'd never heard before concerning Bax's lawyer. We ended up exchanging more messages that spring—principally about the investigation. Jay remembered other comments that Philip had made about the case, and I was able to share information too, as Myles had talked to Const. Craig Thur, a former lead investigator on Krystal's case, more recently than Philip or Paul had.

As we continued to correspond, and after I spoke to Krystal's stepsister Kari, the situation grew clear: Philip had ardently wanted more attention for Krystal's case. In the mid-nineties, he pushed to have Ronald Bax featured on *America's Most Wanted* and *Unsolved Mysteries*. He believed Bax was still out there, and the family hoped national attention would narrow down his hiding places. By the time I reached the Senyks in 2018, however, Philip's dementia made it too painful for him to discuss Krystal's death. And Paul didn't feel comfortable speaking to us without his brother's consent, which Philip was neurologically unable to give.

Despite these setbacks, Myles and I made plans to visit St. Catharines, where Krystal went to university. We wanted to see her old stomping grounds, the farm in North Pelham where she and her brother Gord grew up, as well as her old high school. Jay and I continued to communicate over the summer of 2019. When I mentioned the visit to him that fall, he said he'd like to meet us. We didn't realize yet that their situation had changed. Philip Senyk had passed away the month before. Jay and Paul had flown to Whitehorse and buried Philip beside Krystal at Grey Mountain Cemetery. In late November 2019, a week before Myles and I were due to arrive in St. Catharines, Jay said that he'd spoken to his dad, and they wanted to give us Philip's journals. Given the significance of these notes, and the support this offering represented, their decision moved me. I expected Jay would propose a coffee or beer in town—someplace neutral. When I asked if he recommended a spot, he invited us to his family's farm.

It was dark by the time we found Jay's house on the other side of the canal from where Myles and I were staying in Thorold. We had rented a car in Toronto, where Myles had been attending a work conference, and where I had arrived by train the night before. Jay lived at the far end of a country lane fringed by orchards. As we pulled up to his house, it seemed the only light was what shone from our headlights. Myles saw him before I did—a tall, sturdily built man with a shaved head waving from the front step. He took after Krystal, in that he'd done much of the work on the house himself, including the gazebo, from which you could watch the shipping traffic plod up and down the canal. Because the canal cut through the farmland so narrowly, the freighters looked to be trawling through country fields.

Jay had recently been forced to take time off work to recover from a car wreck. A head injury had compromised his short-term memory, and we spent a portion of that first evening helping him track down the notebooks, which he had tucked away for safekeeping—if only he could remember where. Throughout our weekend together, Jay struck me as thoughtful and kind. He had been the one to organize the burial for his uncle, no small task given the fees and regulations around air travel with human remains. Between his care for Philip while he was alive, his management of the estate now that he'd passed, and care for his own father, who was in hospital for a back operation, many family duties fell on Jay's shoulders. He was also a generous host, taking Myles and me to Niagara Falls the next day, and inviting us for dinner (venison sausages from a deer he had hunted). He didn't seem to mind as we squatted on his floor, sifting through family photos or the album of condolence cards written to Philip, which we found in a plastic storage box in the corner of his basement. We spent hours this way: squinting at Philip's notebooks to decipher his handwriting, gazing at old photos, while Jay's cats, Percey and Bailys, bolted around us or pawed at the manila envelopes. Jay offered memories where he could and opinions on how everything had unfolded. He had been fourteen when Krystal was killed—old enough to feel her loss and to inherit his family's anger.

The "trailer" with some of Krystal's things, it turned out, was a shipping container. It looked like something straight off the docks: a forty-foot sea-can storing all of Philip's belongings. We had to enter without flashlights, because Jay didn't want to alert his aunt in the neighbouring farmhouse. She may not approve of us looking through her brother's things, he explained, though Philip had given Jay legal authority over his estate. We had to wait until we were closed inside the sea-can before Jay turned on the lights. Here we found more of Philip's notebooks and boxes of memorabilia: Krystal's arm wrestling trophies, a Sourdough Rendezvous plaque for her victory in a flour-packing contest. We spent close to an hour in there, identifying folders to take back to the house with us, where we could look through them in greater comfort. We never found diaries or letters, but we discovered more photos—and binders of Philip's notes.

The next day was our last in St. Catharines. Jay wanted to take us back to the Falls for the firework display (it was my birthday), but Myles and I felt increasingly tugged toward the notebooks. In the end, Myles stayed at his Airbnb that day to start reading while I accompanied Jay to Mississauga to visit Paul in the hospital. This is strange to admit, but I felt it my duty to go with him. Not "duty" like "chore." It felt urgent to me. The only way to find Krystal was to meet the ones who loved her. Not to gain information— the information somehow felt secondary to this rite of sitting with them, witnessing anything they wanted to share. It felt like the least I could do, as an interloper in their lives.

Given our truncated communication the year before—Paul literally screening my calls—I wasn't sure how he would receive me. So I felt some relief when Jay woke his father from a nap and Paul blinked at us to say, "An angel!" He proceeded to call the nurses angels too, listing, to all of us, Jay's selling points as a bachelor (at one point calling me his future daughter-in-law, which made Jay and I both squirm, but Paul had said it kindly. He dealt in a currency of charm). We didn't talk too much about the case, or the book, but that didn't matter to me. It felt special simply to meet Paul—to connect with someone Krystal had loved and who loved her in return.

It took three hours to drive back to St. Catharines, owing to commuter traffic slugging out of Toronto. Paul had given us permission to go into his house and search through his home videos—to watch them on his VCR. Myles met us there. It was after seven, and we hadn't stopped for lunch or dinner. All Jay could find in his dad's kitchen were tins of tuna—which we declined, and which he proceeded to eat, one after the other. It was one of those moments that might have felt strange in another context, but given the chain of events that dropped me into the middle of this living room, nothing felt "odd." I accepted all without question.

Paul's home looked like a natural history museum. A great horned owl swooped down the hall beside a red-tailed hawk, which gripped a squirrel in its talons. In the living room, a second great horned owl perched on a tree branch. A snowy owl sat between him and the head of a deer. The walls hosted an assembly of heads: in addition to the deer, there was a moose head, a caribou head, and the head of a 325-pound black bear. A 64-inch moose rack decked the wall to the left of the front door. The living room didn't feel alive per se, but crowded and pelted and plumed, with many sets of eyes on us.

Jay inserted a videotape. I held my breath—I couldn't help but think: This is the moment I get to meet her. To see her move for the first time. To hear the texture of her voice. I settled on a footstool as close as I could to the TV without blocking Myles's and Jay's view. My heart drubbed in my chest.

"It don't look bad to me!"

Philip stands before a luggage carousel. He looks to be in his fifties and wears a crisp short-sleeved shirt. A broad polka-dot tie descends from his collar. It's September 1990. Phil, Krystal's uncle Paul, and their friend Lenny have all flown in from Ontario.

"Wait a minute, I gotta back up to get it all in," laughs Paul behind the camera. The shot pans out to reveal the full length of

Phil's tie, which dangles beyond the crotch of his chinos.

So this was her family: the type who flies across the country in clown ties—to emblazon an inside joke on their chests, or embarrass their twenty-eight-year-old at the airport. I felt instantly fond.

Philip slings his arm around a third man, slightly shorter and thicker in the torso. "This is my friend Lenny," he announces.

"Just take over, it's running," Paul says behind the camera as Philip and Lenny turn to fetch their luggage from the carousel. "See right now it says 'Record' inside?"

"Oh yeah," says a woman. Krystal. We hear her voice before we see her.

The next moment, Paul appears before the camera. He wears aviator sunglasses and a white T-shirt that clings to his chest and biceps. There appears to be a grizzly on the front, but it's hard to see beyond his own paddle-length tie—this one pink with white dots.

"Now it's working," he proclaims. "We'll go over here and pick up my suitcase."

"Maybe take the tie off," Krystal calls. The tie flaps across his stomach as he wanders into the crowd at the carousel.

"That's enough of this now," she mutters. The camera points to the tiled floor, then the ceiling, then the airport's windows as she tries to shut it off.

The next shot reveals Krystal on her truck, a white Ford pickup. The sun beats behind her as she stands in the cargo bed to haul up suitcases. The wind blows wisps of hair across her face. ("Look at the pipes on her," Jay says behind me. And it's true. She looks like a minor god up there, or a wrestler.)

"Just start aiming, that's all," Paul coaches his brother, who's now behind the camera. Paul stands next to the truck, holding a duffle bag for his niece.

"Aim at the ceiling like I did," Krystal laughs.

"Krystal does a good job of aiming at the ceiling," says Paul.

"This is Paul loading the bags into Krystal's truck," narrates Phil. While Paul sounds warm, showman-like, Philip could be dictating a nuclear preparedness video. "We are now in the Yukon," he proclaims.

Krystal waves from the truck toward someone off-screen. They must have commented on the clown ties, for Paul says to the camera, "I don't think they've seen too many gentlemen with ties out here, the way we have so many compliments."

"Look at the tie on that man," says Phil, angling the lens at his brother's chest.

Paul fixes his tie, which was wagging out from his armpit. "Wait a minute, I better stand way back here for you to get it," he says, inching backward.

"Paul, let me have a view of that truck," says Phil.

"It's my truck and I'm almost thirty and he's complaining," says Krystal.

The next shot gazes out the windshield at the black spruce trees crouched along the side of the highway. We glimpse Krystal behind the wheel, one hand steering, her left arm pointing out snow on the mountains.

Paul exclaims from behind the camera: "Wow, look at that, that guy is skiing! Look at that! Right there on the main road! He's skiing!"

On the other side of the highway, a roller-skier strides up the pavement.

Then finally, they're at the cabin. Krystal stands in front of her home. Beyond her, we see a generous porch roofed with sheet metal, a red cylinder in the background—possibly the water pump or water heater.

"All this, this whole stretch here, is a bear reduction zone," she tells the camera, as well as her dad and Lenny, who are out of the frame. "So I can go in and take one grizzly and two black bears a year. There's tons of coyote over there," she adds, pronouncing it "ky-oat."

She wears a lavender tank top tucked into blue jeans, her figure tall and strong-looking. Two of her king shepherds nose the dirt by her feet. Behind her, flags of laundry whistle out from a clothesline.

"Well, Mum, this is Krystal's place," announces Paul off-screen. He steps back, revealing his brother a few feet away next to the pickup truck. Philip's gaze follows his daughter's toward the end of her property. A glow of pride blooms across his cheeks.

"Yeah, it goes out the front there for two and a half acres," Krystal says.

"Where's your water here?" asks Philip, turning to her.

"Listen," she says. "You hear it?"

There's an ambient hum, belonging to the water pump, the creek, or maybe Paul's VCR.

"Yeah," he says.

"That's it."

Next, Paul revolves the camera to reveal a table saw, push mower, and canoe banked in the grass. With the sun at this angle, the meadow is effulgent. A crease of black spruce marks the rear of Krystal's property, and beyond that, the smooth-sloping hills.

"See my garden?" she says. They amble toward a fertile patch fenced with wire. "This is all mine."

"Oh!" booms Paul. "Got a little bit of everything! Potatoes, beets, onions, carrots. *Beans!* Little bit of everything."

"Can't have much of a growing season," says Philip.

"It's short. I put it in June first."

The group meanders toward the back of Krystal's house. Philip still wears his clown tie, the tail of it walloping out from his side as he walks. When they pass a stack of freshly hewn logs, he mumbles something to his daughter.

Krystal protests: "Oh, I can't carry that myself! You try picking up one of those things!"

They reach the greenhouse she built, a modest frame walled with sheets of soft plastic.

"What have we got in here, Krystal?" asks Paul.

"Four or five different kinds of tomatoes. We got beans, parsley . . ."

"Oh Phil, look at this," interrupts Paul from behind the camera. "You just walk in and you pick a—oh!"

Philip's hand reaches into the shot, plucking a fat, crimson bauble. "Paul, here, look at that. This is a—"

"A Krystal tomato!" Paul interrupts.

Krystal laughs in the background.

"A Yukon tomato," says Philip. "Watch, watch." He lifts the tomato to his mouth and bites contemplatively. "Oh—yum! Yum! Yum!" he repeats, shaking his head in appreciation.

"*Hey*! That was my only tomato."

Later, they climb the steps to her back porch, which she also built herself.

"That's a way into the basement," she says, indicating a small door off the side.

"You have like a root cellar?" asks Lenny.

"There's a whole basement underneath."

The door squeaks open, and we see inside her house for the first time: the walls half panelled with wood, half drywalled. A kitchen sits to the right of the back door, the shelves stacked with mason jars. On the opposite side of this main room, a dining table fills the wall. The camera pans to reveal a comfortable seating nook with velour sofas, a picture window, sun ladling in.

"I just started working on this room too," says Krystal, leading her father, uncle, and Lenny into a sunlit extension, wood planks stacked in the middle of the unfinished floor.

The men had flown in from Ontario to go hunting. Krystal's friends Eddy and Suzanne would join them, as they had wilderness training and visitors to the Yukon were required to have local guides for outdoor expeditions. The three of them—Krystal, Eddy, and Suzanne—would guide Paul, Philip, and Lenny in the bush over the next five days.

Jay had given us Suzanne's number, and I called her in December 2019. I told her who I was and why I was phoning. There was a palpable beat of hesitation. Then she said: "I'm sorry, I can't help you. I promised Colleen I wouldn't talk to anyone."

"Oh," I said, dumbly. This wasn't the answer I'd been expecting. Sure, she might decline—I always braced myself for people to decline. But I didn't anticipate this as the reason. "Okay," I said. "I understand."

"I'm sorry," she said. And she sounded like she was.

Myles had contacted Colleen in January 2015, when he first learned about Krystal's story. Colleen replied with one line: "Please do not contact me about this again." Three years later, when Myles and I began working together, I tried myself. At the very least, Colleen needed to know that we were planning to write a book. For several days, I chewed over the most courteous way to approach her. I wanted to respect her boundaries, but at the same time notify her of our plans. Ideally, I wanted to hear her side of the story, if she was willing to share. In the end, I wrote an old-fashioned letter, on paper, with the hope it might convey some of the sensitivity and respect I felt in approaching her. I explained who I was, how I had learned about Krystal, and our intentions for the book. Finally, I asked if she would be willing to speak with me, mentioning that I would be visiting the Yukon that August.

I never heard back. As my flight to Whitehorse loomed closer, I sent the letter by email as well, in case we'd used an outdated mailing address. Again, I never heard back. I thought about what dogged journalists do in these situations, like John Vaillant, who knocked on the door of his more elusive interview subject while writing *The Golden Spruce*. Ultimately, neither Myles nor I had the heart to do that. In one night, Colleen lost the father of her boys as well as her best friend; no wonder she didn't want to revisit that experience.

A year after we spoke on the phone, Suzanne got back in touch. Her ex-husband, who still lived in the Yukon, had passed along Myles's contact information. She emailed Myles, saying that she'd thought hard about it over the past year, and she would like to talk about what happened. In fact, she needed to. She said that Colleen's silence had been to protect her sons, who were both in their thirties now. As adults, "they should be able to handle the information they probably know anyway," Suzanne reasoned. "They'll likely see the book. I'd rather you didn't get all your information from somebody who might skew it one way. But the main reason [to talk to you] is that I need to do it for myself. I have let Colleen know this. I need to talk about it."

Suzanne had also come from around St. Catharines. While she was still living there, her father read an article in the local newspaper about a young woman who resided in the Yukon during the winter, then passed her summers in Ontario. Suzanne couldn't stop thinking about this story—how this woman, Colleen, spent her winters so far north, the opposite season most people would choose. Suzanne started work at a local farm and discovered that, by coincidence, Colleen was working there too. They started chatting. Within days of getting to know each other, Suzanne decided to move to the Yukon too. Colleen said she was going back at the end of the summer. When Suzanne asked how, Colleen said she would hitchhike. Suzanne said she had a car—did she want a ride? That's all it took. They drove out together in 1981 and had been friends ever since.

Krystal and Colleen had been close since their school days. When Krystal followed Colleen to the territory in the mid-1980s, Suzanne got to know her too. Often, when Ron was away on hunting trips, Suzanne would stay with Colleen and the kids. That's how Suzanne first met Krystal, in 1988. Krystal was going hunting with Ron, an overnight trip in the Northwest Territories. They were both still at the house when Suzanne arrived. Right away Krystal struck Suzanne as "vivacious, full of life, obviously very smart, and gorgeous." After Ron and Krystal left, Suzanne asked her friend: "Aren't you worried?"

Colleen said, "No, because I trust Krystal."

This was the first time Ron and Krystal had gone hunting together. When they returned, something had ruptured between them. We don't know what happened on that trip, but from that point forward, they hated each other.

Suzanne recalled the friendship dynamics of that time: "Krystal and Colleen were the main good friends," she said, though she never felt like the odd person out. "I was busy with my own life. At times we'd all get together, or I would hang out with Colleen, or just Krystal."

She and Krystal would hike together—they both loved the outdoors. Suzanne saw Krystal as a strong, "self-made woman," and she considered herself to be similar. Once, Krystal, Suzanne, and Suzanne's three-year-old son, David, piled into Krystal's truck to pick up some chickens from a neighbour in Carcross. Krystal took a shortcut up a steep hill, on a road that no one else travelled on. It was mid-winter, and they ended up getting stuck. They had to spend the night on that hill. It was minus thirty-five outside—cold enough for them to freeze to death. Krystal had some big mitts sewn from leather and fur, and she put them on David's feet to keep him warm. She also had candles in the truck, for emergencies like this, and they lit them.

"You wouldn't think we could laugh about that, but we did," Suzanne remembered. "We felt it was a big adventure. We didn't feel scared—it wasn't like we were out in the boondocks. We were in some back corner of town. We thought, well, let's just stay here the night and figure it out the next morning. Of course, we were young then. Getting the chickens—that was an adventure."

She described how the chickens were in awful condition, soggy, their wings slick with excrement. When Colleen picked one up, the bird slapped her in the face with a "very wet and shitty wing." Krystal couldn't stop laughing.

The photos from the hunting trip they all took together show Krystal in canvas waders fastened by suspenders. Her teal shirt is spotless compared to the waders, which are mottled with mud, soot, and fish guts. In one photo, Krystal stands with her arm around Philip in a plaid coat. They're almost the same height. Behind them, a lake reflects citrus-yellow trees. In another, she poses with Paul and Suzanne before a giant set of antlers. Paul stands in the centre with a bandana cinched around his hairline. They're all grinning loudly.

Paul, Philip, and Lenny had tags for moose and bear, though they never caught any on this excursion—only fish. (One tag entitles the hunter to target one particular animal.) When they set up their base camp on the first day, the guys from Ontario fixated on building a shelter from an abandoned tent frame. Krystal and Suzanne had teased the "southern boys" about this, but when the weather turned, the more luxurious shelter came in handy. On the last day of the trip, they left the area by float plane. The men took the first trip out, while Krystal and Suzanne waited with the gear. They stood on a rock near the water, chatting, enjoying the sun on their skin, when a raven swooped overhead and eliminated on Suzanne—icing the right side of her face, hair, and shoulder. Krystal laughed so hard she was immobilized, leaving her friend to rinse the splat out of her hair herself.

That seemed to be the thread among these photos, videos, and stories: laughter. Joy in its rawest, involuntary form.

5.

DOMESTIC

When Suzanne used to drop by Colleen and Ron's house for a visit, she'd always find Ron in the basement. She'd ask how he was doing, and he'd show her the latest sculpture in progress. It would occur to her, as they chatted, how poisonous the air must be. He used so many chemicals in his projects, you could hardly breathe down there. She wondered what that did, over time, to a person's brain. But she liked Ron: he was nice, and a talented artist. As an outdoors person herself, she admired his ability to spend so much solo time in the wilderness. Now and then, Colleen would hint to Suzanne, "You only see one side of him," or "You don't know what he's really like." For a long time, Colleen kept details of the abuse to herself.

For the most part, Ron was good with their sons. He loved them and felt proud to be a family man. Once, when he was working construction, he was driving a steamroller down Two Mile Hill in Whitehorse. The brakes failed, and he began careering out of control. All he could think was that he might kill a child, so he veered into the ditch, risking his own life instead.

Another time, when Colleen was heavily pregnant, he asked her to come with him to retrieve an antler for carving. What he didn't tell her was the deer had been freshly slain by a grizzly, which meant the bear was likely lingering in the area. When they arrived at the carcass, Colleen realized the situation and gave him hell for bringing her (and their unborn child) to a fresh kill.

Their dog snatched off into the trees. When he bounded back to the clearing, a grizzly was charging after him. Ron tried to shoot with his rifle, but the bear tackled him—knocking him down, its jaws inches from Ron's face. He managed to wrestle the gun into the bear's mouth and pull the trigger.

Colleen was furious. Ron was so cocky, he could have gotten them all killed. It was also a waste of the grizzly's life. The bear was only trying to protect its food.

It was when her sons started to mimic Ron, echoing his hideous words to her, that she decided to leave. They separated the day after Christmas in 1991. Ron was devastated. He didn't have many friends he could confide in, so he began talking to Suzanne. He wasn't the type to show his vulnerability, so it felt pretty momentous when he broke down in front of her. She did her best to listen.

She hadn't understood Colleen's intimations that she saw only one side of Ron until she witnessed his violence herself. It was Valentine's Day 1992—two weeks before Krystal's murder. Colleen had asked Suzanne to help her collect their belongings from the house. Ron wasn't supposed to be there, but he showed up as they were packing. Colleen was crouched on the floor, stuffing clothes into a bag. Ron bent over her, shouting, spewing terrible names. He began throwing things at them—potted plants, then a chair. They fled from the house. Colleen was borrowing Krystal's truck, and they locked the doors as he lurched after them, slamming his palms on the hood, yelling at them to get out of the vehicle. Suzanne stared through the windshield in disbelief. He was unrecognizable. Colleen had tried to tell her for years that there was this side to him; she realized she should have taken those comments more seriously. Finally, he let go. Colleen barrelled the truck out of the driveway. How much of their marriage had Colleen lived this way? Suzanne felt awful. For Ron too. It rent her heart to see two people she cared for in so much pain.

The first time I watched the law skirt the edges of private life was during a trip to New York. I was nineteen, one of thirty students from the University of Victoria in town for the National Model United Nations conference, where university delegations represent UN member states in mock councils, committees, and assemblies. I had signed up mostly for the opportunity to go to New York, and because at that time I still wanted to be a lawyer.

That year, UVic represented the Republic of Korea, and I was to sit on the Commission on Crime Prevention and Criminal Justice. If you're wondering what a fake UN committee looks like, picture a conference room of shiny undergraduate students in blazers: they wave their placards, speak from the podium, shake hands, and beetle into corners to draft resolutions on someone's laptop.

On the evening of the first day, I excused myself from a delegation meeting to scheme with the Netherlands. Around seven, I left the hotel room of our faculty advisor and tried to find the elevator. The hallways were relatively vacant—everyone at dinner or colluding in their rooms. I had just about determined where I was going when I saw a woman's feet in high heels being dragged around the corner, the bulbs of her pumps imprinting the carpet.

A delegate from another university strode down the hall in the same direction. She glanced at the scene, whatever was going on, and hurried into her room. I hastened my pace. When I turned the corner, I found a woman lying on her back. Her arms stretched above her head, grasped by a man who looked to be in his thirties. The man was not tall, but he had a muscle mass I would describe as burly, and a goatee. I took one look at the man, then the woman, and asked the woman if she was okay.

She could barely keep her eyes open. She didn't appear distressed, but she looked out of it. It was hard to imagine this mode of transport was consensual.

"We're okay," the man answered. "My wife had too much to drink at the bar."

I looked at him again, and I looked back at the woman. He had let go of one of her arms, but she continued to lay on the floor, saliva budding at the corner of her lip.

I held eye contact. "Do you want to come with me to my room?"

She nodded. I stretched out my hand, and she reached for it.

"Thanks for your concern," the man said, jerking her back toward him. "We're fine. She just had a bit too much to drink." He began opening the door to his room.

"I'm not asking you," I said.

I looked back to the woman, who was trying to sit up. "Do you want to come with me?"

She said yes. I crouched to help her stand.

But the man had his door open now. He was tugging her inside.

"She wants to come with me," I said.

"Thank you, we don't need your help," he said, both our voices now raised.

Again, I tried to help the woman off the floor. He yanked her toward him, and uselessly, I began pulling in the opposite direction. We struggled over the threshold of his room, the woman's arms splayed between us. It occurred to me this couldn't be comfortable for her, and that we might both end up in his room. When his pager popped off his belt, I let go. He fell back, with the woman, across the threshold. I snatched the pager off the floor, noted the room number, and scurried back to my faculty advisor's room.

We called security. Over the phone I told them what happened. Twenty or thirty minutes later, they knocked on my door.

They thanked me for letting them know, but there was nothing they could do. "It's a domestic," they explained.

"A domestic?" I repeated, not comprehending why they weren't down there now, doing something.

"They're married."

I still didn't get it. So what if they were married? He was dragging her by the wrist.

"She had too much to drink at the bar," they told me.

"She looked drugged."

"There's nothing we can do," they repeated, "as it's a domestic."

Again, this word puzzled me. I knew about intimate partner violence, and I knew the law could step in. I recalled, hazily, the divine right of kings, where the monarch is subject to no earthly authority. Was there a divine right of husbands? Were the earthly authorities too embarrassed or indifferent to step in? And how did the security guards know they were married? Because the man said so?

They must have mistaken my confusion for disappointment, for they said, "It's okay, you had reason to be concerned. You did the right thing."

Then it occurred to me that the couple *may* have been married. That she *may* have had too much to drink. That I'd interfered when it was none of my business. I felt a wriggle of guilt, or embarrassment. But an equal wriggle said: Do non-abusive husbands drag their intoxicated wives down the hall? And: *she wanted to come with me.*

I was still clutching the man's pager: a lump of heavy plastic with a metal clip on the side. No one used pagers anymore, I thought, except doctors and drug dealers. Maybe not even doctors.

"I have his pager," I told the security guards.

They took the device from me and wished me a pleasant evening.

In 2012, the leader of the Yukon New Democratic Party, Elizabeth Hanson, wrote a letter to the editor of the *Yukon News*. She had been a friend and colleague of Krystal Senyk.

> Twenty years on, I wonder if we have learned anything from the countless Krystals who have died in this country as a result of domestic disputes gone terribly awry. Died because the police could not or would not take seriously the level of threat or danger that a woman can face in the complex web that domestic violence weaves.
>
> And I wonder, as I did the day I had to tell my daughters that Krystal was dead, that she had been killed because she was trying to help her friend, how I would answer them today if they asked, as they did that day: "Mommy, does that mean if I help a friend that I might get killed?"[1]

Hanson's concerns remain as relevant today—another ten years on—as ever. The word I want to interrogate, or cut open and root to the bottom of, is *domestic*. The word *domestic* comes from the Latin *domus*, a house style in ancient Rome and the "domain" of a household more broadly. In Roman domestic law, the home was recognized as *commune perfugium*, a (free, land-owning) man's "common asylum," or *perfugium sanctum*, a sacred haven. Even to bring a man to court, the law could not enter his personal sanctuary. Cicero wrote:

> What is holier and more strongly fortified by all religious law than the house of each and every citizen? . . . Here

are the altars, here the hearths, here the [household gods],
here the sacred things, reverence, rituals are contained.
This refuge is so holy for everyone that it is never right to
snatch anyone away from there.[2]

As master of the house, or paterfamilias, the husband would
have legal reign over his dependants, including his wife, children,
relatives, servants, and slaves. (The word *familia* originally meant a
group of *famuli*, or slaves.) He had authority, called *manus* (hand),
over his wife, whose body and property he owned. Because he was
legally responsible for her actions, he had the right to punish, sell,
or kill his wife as he deemed prudent, even if he rarely exercised it.

More recently, the phrase "rule of thumb" has been attributed
to a statement by eighteenth-century judge Sir Francis Buller, who
pronounced that a man was allowed to beat his wife with a stick
no thicker than his thumb. Though this origin story has come into
question, English common law did allow husbands to beat their
wives—a legal allowance called chastisement—and the phrase
has been widely adopted, including in a 1982 report on domestic
violence published by the US Commission on Civil Rights titled
"Under the Rule of Thumb."

Manus and *thumb*. It's morphologically interesting, if grim,
that these metaphors invoke hands, the prevailing weapon in intimate partner violence.

Domus, home, is the root, also, of *dominate*.

Our legal system has nominally moved beyond such precepts,
although a presumption of the home's inviolability remains. For
the most part, this is a good thing. It has been used to support the
basic privacy of citizens, as well as sexual rights ("There's no place
for the state in the bedrooms of the nation," said then prime minister Pierre Trudeau in 1967). But this presumed inviolability has
also been levied as an excuse for non-intervention.

"There's nothing we can do. It's a domestic," the New York security guards said to me. "The police can't really get involved in cases of domestic disputes," the constable told Colleen and Krystal at the transition home in Whitehorse. They could have been quoting Cicero's speech directly: *non domus, commune perfugium*.

Liberal democracies consider the private realm hermetic: "personal, intimate, autonomous, particular, individual, the original source and final outpost of the self," writes Catharine MacKinnon.[3] Injuries arise when outside forces violate our inner sanctum, not forces within the sanctum itself. When the law centres privacy as a right, the burden of scrutiny is dispersed. The eye of law enforcement looks askance, toward more visible problems. To be more precise: when the law centres privacy as a right within a patriarchal system, violence committed by men at home is more likely to gain impunity. Spousal rape wasn't even criminalized in Canada until 1983, and even now, most cases tend to stay out of the legal system. Privacy itself isn't the problem—it's the frame we're embedded in.

Coverture is the legal term for a man's domination over his wife, another principle established by English common law, which remained in effect until the late nineteenth century. Upon marriage, man and woman would merge into one entity. Her property, rights, and legal status would be absorbed, amoeba-like, into her husband's. Under the same laws, an adult unmarried woman was labelled a feme sole, who had the right to own property or sign contracts, while a married woman was called a feme covert, an anglicized misspelling of *femme couverte*, or "covered woman," whose "very being or legal existence . . . is suspended during the marriage, or at least is incorporated and consolidated into that of the husband."[4]

A married woman could not own property, sign contracts, earn her own salary, or go to school without her husband's permission.

Until relatively recently, marriage rites functioned as a legal disappearing act. Though married women in England, the United States, and Canada saw more rights under the law starting in the late nineteenth century, the aftertaste of coverture and other misogynist doctrines lingers. Myrna Dawson, the director of the Canadian Femicide Observatory for Justice and Accountability, used the phrase "intimacy discount" to express how men who murder their partners receive lighter penalties than those who kill strangers. Convictions on charges related to intimate partner violence are rare, Dawson told *Maclean's* in the magazine's 2019 investigation into domestic violence.[5] In the hundreds of cases Dawson took to court in the preceding eight years, only one made it to trial. "Typically, the Crown withdraws the charges and the defendant enters into a peace bond after completion of a partner-assault response program," writes Anne Kingston, the author of the article. "That means no trial, no sentencing, no criminal record."[6]

As Philip Senyk followed his daughter's murder investigation, he repeatedly expressed concerns that even if they caught Ronald Bax, the courts would likely go easy on him. In November 1995, three years after Krystal's murder, and 120 kilometres north, Ralph Klassen strangled his wife, Susan, with both hands and a ligature. Klassen claimed "provocation" as a defence, due to the "negative comments" his wife made, which "insulted his manhood" and drove him into a "deep, blind rage."[7] In December 1996, Klassen was convicted of manslaughter and sentenced to five years in prison, eligible for parole by 1998.[8] He was released in May 2000, after serving two-thirds of his sentence. (This "statutory release" has been required by law since 1992, replacing historic releases based on "good behaviour.")

The judicial blotting out of intimate partner violence suggests that courts believe a violent husband or boyfriend poses less threat to the general public than someone whose violent acts are more random. French philosopher René Girard has written on sacred violence: how societies have used ritual to channel social crises, such as disease and famine, into a sacrificial victim. The victim would provide an outlet and container for the threat. The justice system works a bit this way: we put wrongdoers behind bars in an attempt to contain crime, even if the reasons for crime are socially rooted, not traceable to any one individual. We try the perpetrator (through a public "hearing" and witnessing of their wrongs) to prevent further harm, as well as to bring resolution for the victims and their families. Legal scholar Brian R. Decker applies Girard's model to intimate partner violence, suggesting that the legal system hesitates to penalize abusive men because law enforcers tacitly view the victims as sacrifices that contain social violence within the home, where it is less threatening to the public.[9] We tolerate ordered (contained, "domestic") violence because it tempers disordered (un-contained, public) violence—all on a tacit, concealed level, of course.

According to the Canadian Femicide Observatory, a woman or girl is killed every other day in our country. A woman is killed by her male partner once a week.[10] Of all police-reported violent crimes in Canada, intimate partner violence accounts for one-quarter of them.[11] Nearly half (48 percent) of all solved homicides involving a female victim were committed by her spouse or intimate partner.[12] As reported by the World Health Organization, 30 percent of women around the world have experienced intimate partner violence or non-partner sexual violence at least once in their life.[13] Not surprisingly, violence against trans people is even more pervasive. The 2015 U.S. Transgender Survey found that more than 54 percent of respondents had experienced intimate partner violence, and 47 percent had been sexually assaulted.[14]

Men experience violence too—in Canada, one in five cases of intimate partner violence include a male victim.[15] But men are also the majority of the perpetrators.

Given the rates of intimate partner and gender-based violence, Decker's proposal that our society sacrifices thousands of lives each year may not be as outrageous as it sounds. I depart from Decker's theory when he suggests that we're doing so with inference of ritual. If not always seen or public, ritual is mindful, a solemn sequence of actions. The rates of gender-based violence suggest, if anything, radical indifference.

When a dominant power causes harm, we tend to call it not "violence," but "law and order." When individuals cause harm—especially if we perceive them as "outside" society or rogue—we criminalize their actions, suggesting their behaviour is aberrant. When individuals cause harm inside their own homes, we tend to not speak about it, even if we know it goes on. Despite its ubiquity on all scales of society, it's tempting to view such violence as none of our business—that which happens to other people. This is a comfort, for some. It makes us feel safer and less complicit.

Wolf-Dieter Narr states that "as soon as one begins to determine the term [violence], and as soon as one tries to be precise, to limit its aspects, dimensions and meanings, one faces the danger of covering up [other instances]."[16] Often, we focus on physical evidence of harm—material facts or traces. A bruise. Blood. A fistful of hair.

Narr proposes a "cautionary conclusion" that may serve as "an adequate beginning":

> There *can be* and there *should not be* a clear-cut definition of what violence is all about. Such a clear-cut definition would not enable us to come to grips with the multi-headed, labyrinthine-like intriguing phenomenon of violence.[17]

I like this non-definition. Violence as multi-headed. Irreducible. A labyrinth. Narr acknowledges the dangers of not defining violence: the term can become acritical, unusable for analysis. If everyone may devise their own concept of violence, does the word lose meaning?

I propose: no. As the nature of violence defies precision, the word will not lose meaning if we define it as multiple. We might understand violence as a force—physical or otherwise—and sometimes as the absence of force, as negligence, or concealment. Also, denial. Injury. Distortion. Violation. Destruction. From the Latin *vis* ("strength" or "force"), shaded by *volo* ("I will"). Violence as shoving. Punching. Slapping. Insults. Slurs. Shaming. Negging. Obsession. Threats. Unbroken eye contact. Boiling water. Firearms. Knives. Hands. Fists. Words. Feet. Boots. Belts. Rope. Duct tape. Gossip. Photos. Blackmail. Bleach. Opiates. Methamphetamines. Sexploitation. Screwdrivers. Axes. Doors. Walls. Pots. Frying pans. Plates. Fryer oil. Ashtrays. Cigarettes. Lighter fluid. Gasoline. Brooms. Pillows. Extension cords. Duvet covers. Scissors. Bottles. Irons. Cars. Rape. Slut-shaming. Gaslighting. Scapegoating.

An incomplete list.

Though no evidence suggests that Krystal was gay, Ronald Bax propagated rumours about her relationship with Colleen, which contributed to a disturbing local discourse that she "deserved it."

In the days after the murder, local activist Helen Fallding stated: "This week I can't help but know that yes, there are violent men in the Yukon, and yes, there are men who hate women for being strong and being independent and being strong for other women."[18] She commented on the homophobia she'd experienced in the community, saying it felt "absurd and incongruous, almost laughable" that anyone had a problem with her being a lesbian. In

Toronto, Fallding could focus on other causes, like saving whales if she wanted, because her sexual orientation wasn't something she had to fight for daily. After moving to the Yukon, her fight for gay rights had "taken over."

"It can be really, really awful here," Fallding told the *Yukon News.* "I've met a lot of Yukoners who tell violent anti-gay jokes and think they're funny. I believe that if I got killed they'd think it was sad. But there'd always be that but. 'But I kind of deserved it. But I was gay.'"[19]

At an event for International Women's Day, days after Krystal's murder, Helen Fallding received the Wonderful Woman Award for activism. She accepted the award on behalf of her "lesbian sisters":

Both those who live their love openly and those who
don't yet find it safe to be honest with you. Every strong,
independent woman who stands up for other women is
eventually accused of being a lesbian. Until there is no
more harassment and discrimination against lesbians, no
woman is free to choose how she lives.[20]

She acknowledged all the women in the territory who refused to be silenced, including Krystal Senyk. "As an activist, I can't celebrate tonight," Fallding said at the end of her speech. "I can't put aside or postpone my grief—because Krystal is someone that I knew—and I can't set aside my anger." The button on her chest said, *Silence is the voice of complicity.*[21]

A month later, in a presentation to the Canadian Panel on Violence Against Women, Fallding's partner, Lisa Tremblay, spoke on behalf of the Lesbian Issues Committee of the Yukon Status of Women Council. "I will be brief and I will be blunt," she began. "Women who love women are not physically safe in this territory. The threat of violence keeps us silent."[22] She described the organized anti-gay hatred she had witnessed, such as six or seven years earlier when the Yukon proposed including sexual orientation in its human rights act and hate letters swarmed the local papers.

"My partner got an award on International Women's Day this year for being a lesbian activist," Tremblay went on. "It's nice to be recognized, but ever since then, we've had hang-up calls at home almost every day. Six weeks later a caller finally spoke. He said: 'I just want you to fuck off out of this fucking town or you're fucking in trouble. I mean it.'"[23]

She explained that citizens who receive threats are supposed to turn to the police, and that they'd tried that. But police officers were twice as likely as the men on the street to hate them. When they began receiving hang-up calls, the police told them they couldn't do anything unless there was a threat—a familiar refrain. When the threat arrived, the RCMP promised to install a trace on the line, but forgot. The next call wasn't tracked. By the time they set up a trace, the calls had stopped. Tremblay recalled another incident where a local movie theatre screened a film with a gay theme. A heterosexual woman called the RCMP for security, because she worried the event would attract negative attention from homophobes. The first officer she spoke to said he didn't like gays, that he didn't have to like them, and he didn't care what happened to them. When she asked to speak to another officer, she got a moderately more cordial version of the same message.

"Heterosexual women need to understand that anti-lesbian violence can also affect them," Tremblay stated in her speech. "Any woman who is independent, physically strong or supportive of her female friends will eventually get labelled a dyke. It's standard for abusive men to use accusations of lesbianism to keep their partners in line."[24]

Like Fallding a month earlier, Tremblay mentioned Krystal's murder, how Yukon women were living in fear. Some abusive partners were even using her murder as a threat, warning that if their wife or girlfriend didn't comply, they would end up like Krystal Senyk.

"Many Yukoners believe Krystal deserved to die," Tremblay said. "Or at the very least to get hurt. The reasons people give vary. But a common one is that she is rumoured to have been a lesbian. That it's okay to shoot lesbians is supposed to be self-explanatory."[25]

Another resident of Whitehorse recalled the atmosphere after Krystal's murder. One of her co-workers hung a framed photo of Ronald Bax on the wall, with the word "HERO" pinned underneath. Her (exclusively male) colleagues thought it was hilarious. This was part of the homophobia and sexual harassment she experienced daily at work. She was the only woman working at the TV studio, the only one with formal training, and the lowest paid.

However Krystal would describe her sexual orientation, Bax's rage was fuelled by the belief that she was engaging in a relationship with his wife. These rumours set the tone for how her murder would be rationalized by some in the community. For them, Krystal had gone out of bounds. As a woman who reconstructed her own house, who hunted grizzly bears, who was a champion arm-wrestler, who worked as an engineer—she was trespassing outside her role as "woman." As a sisterly friend to Colleen, a friend who moved across the country after Colleen did, who bought a house nearby, who served as a surrogate aunt for Colleen's children, driving them to daycare or the medical clinic—she was trespassing outside her role as "friend." By both counts, she was encroaching on Ronald Bax's territory. At least, that's how he read the situation. And he wasn't the only one.

"The police can't really get involved in cases of domestic disputes," the constable told Colleen in the smoking room of the transition home. She had just shown him the threat she'd written down on a tissue: *the hunt is on*. She told the constable that Ron had really flipped this time, and that he possessed a collection of guns. As the transition home staff knew in 1992, it is against the law to threaten to kill or seriously harm someone. That's why Colleen's advocate drove her to the police station the next day to press charges— before either of them realized that Bax had made good on his words. When Myles asked Constable Thur about this point over email, he replied:

> Section 264 (1) CC [Criminal Harassment] was not in the Criminal Code in 1992. My assessment of BAX's actions at the time was that this would have been an appropriate charge given his behaviour.

> Section 264.1 CC [Uttering Threats] was in the Criminal Code in 1992, however threats would have needed to have been clear and specific and they would have had to have been reported to the police in order for charges to be laid.

I suppose "the hunt is on. The hunt begins tomorrow. Oh forget it, I'm on my way," spoken by a career hunter who owned a collection of rifles was not adequately "clear and specific." Shortly after Krystal's murder, Jan Forde, the director of the transition home, told the *Whitehorse Star*: "People think someone has to follow through on these acts before they can do anything. I think sometimes the police don't understand, or are not always willing to respond."[26]

According to the article, certain people in Whitehorse and Carcross were commenting that Krystal "got what she deserved" for "interfering" in Colleen and Ron's marriage. "It's much easier to blame a woman for a man's action than to blame the man," said Forde. RCMP Corporal Dan Otterbein responded, saying the RCMP was more than willing to investigate someone uttering threats, so long as the threats were substantiated and within the guidelines of the Criminal Code. "We can't investigate what we don't know," he commented. "People have to trust police and assist us with following through on the investigation."

And when police do know? When there's still no investigation? Or no investigation until someone gets killed?

In 1992, the relevant Criminal Code section read like this:

Uttering threats

264.1 (1) Every one commits an offence who, in any

manner, knowingly utters, conveys or causes any person

to receive a threat

(a) to cause death or bodily harm to any person

Compare this section to Ron's words: *The hunt is on. The hunt begins tomorrow. Oh forget it, I'm on my way.*

I struggle to see how his threat evades the definition. Did he need to say "you"? "I'm going to hunt *you* down"? Given the officer didn't jot down a single note until Krystal corrected him about Bax's vehicle, I'm unconvinced he was evaluating Bax's omission of pronouns.

On April 14, 1992, ten days before the above-mentioned article in the *Whitehorse Star*, the same journalist, Sherryl Yeager, reported about a man charged with threatening to kill his wife and children earlier that year. He had pled guilty in January, and in April was sentenced to a further three months in prison, in addition to three years probation, with an order to undergo residential treatment, anger management classes, psychological and psychiatric assessment, treatment, and follow-up counselling. The court also mandated that he submit blood tests, attend Alcoholics Anonymous, and not contact his wife or her sister, nor see his children, unless authorized by a probation officer. Additionally, he was prohibited from possessing a weapon for five years.

In his thirty-three-page judgment, Judge Barry Stuart said death threats should be taken more seriously by the court. "The strain of death threats for a prolonged period can readily be equated to being imprisoned by fear; an imprisonment that can be more restrictive of basic freedoms and destructive of the enjoyment of life than serving time in jail."[27]

Sadly, the officer who spoke to Krystal and Colleen at the transition home on March 1, 1992, didn't treat Bax's threats with the same gravity.

"Maybe you can call the cops in Carcross," Krystal had suggested.

But the police in Carcross were "doing their own thing" that night. "There's nothing we can do in domestic relationships," the constable repeated. "We have to wait until he breaks the law."

6.

MONUMENT

Philip's journals run from March 2, 1992, to sometime in 2015. Typed, they amount to twenty thousand words. The sheer detail of these notes—every phone call to police, every voice message, every empty lead, every lead investigator (six between 1992 and 2015)— archives the agony, dullness, and frustration of a murder investigation unresolved.

The first note, written on the day of Krystal's murder, is disquieting in its simplicity:

March 2, 1992
Approximately 11:30 PM time Julie woke me up and told me my mother was on the phone. I answered and Mother told me that Krystal was dead, that her stepbrother Gordie had went to her place and the Mounties were there and they would not let him go inside.

Next, Philip details the burial arrangements:

March 29, 1992
Bank account info – put in $400 for Krystal headstone downpayment
Plot numbers on the left of Krystal and right no 46 and 48
Krystal's number 47

I will check and see if in the Yukon they put one on top
of other like they do in St. Catharines
Place she is put to rest is Grey Mountain—that is the name

March 31, 1992
Plots for grave site in this book – purchased March 31, 92
I own 46 & 48, Krystal 47
Section 11 – Block D – Plot 46: Phil Senyk
Section 11 – Block D – Plot 48: Paul Senyk

Philip purchased the plots on either side of Krystal so that
her mother, Vera, couldn't claim one: a reflection of their hostile
relations at the time. Several friends and family members describe
Krystal's relationship with Vera as strained. Possibly that contributed to Philip's decision about the cemetery plots, which could
be interpreted as cruel out of context (or maybe even in context).
Other family members suggest that Krystal and her mother were
close in their way: alike in their stubbornness and determination,
as well as their devotion to painting and music. In any case, their
relationship was severed by the murder—unable to heal or evolve.

A week after the March 31 entry, Philip, his second wife, Julie,
and Paul flew to Whitehorse for Krystal's funeral. They stayed
with Suzanne, their guide on the hunting trip eighteen months
earlier. Here, Philip puzzles together the time of Krystal's death.

April 8, 1992
10:45 = left Suzanne = 50 minutes
Get home
Killed 11:30 – 12:00

Many of Philip's notes chronicle the walls he would encounter
as he attempted to obtain official documents from both government

and non-governmental institutions. Reading these entries, I have the sense he is grasping for a shred of closure. Some families of murder victims find resolution by attending the trial, even if the process of resurfacing all that pain, parsing it detail by detail, can be harrowing. It's still a ritual of sorts: lawyers narrativizing the event before judge and jury; the appropriate formality, everyone dressed in suits, if not wigs and robes; the bows before entering or leaving the courtroom; the formal address (*Your Honour*, *Your Lordship*, *Your Ladyship*, *my learned friend*); the crown stamped everywhere, if not the scales of justice—all this contributes to the sense that something grave will unfold, something finally, suitably grave.

Yet with Bax never captured, Philip was denied this ritual resolution. For answers, he turned to documents, such as the final autopsy report, which he wouldn't receive for another year.

May 18, 1993
My daughter Krystal was killed March 1/92. After all the heartache and sleepless nights, trying to get autopsy report. Finally dealt with [coroner] Larry Campbell from Vancouver. He went to Whitehorse for a week and told me all the questions I asked with an honest answer. This man is a gentleman's gentleman – if only all people in need of the truth and to be dealt with fairly could have the fortune to meet a man as I did. Larry Campbell has been just as honest as a good friend. I'm glad to have dealt with him.
After reading the report a few times, the inner self feels empty. Did not read report when I got home, read it after I got myself ready. Just did not open when I got home as I thought I would, when I got it after fighting for it for so long.

As the months ticked by, the entries suggest he found it harder
to trust the institutions charged with answering his questions.

June 28, 1993
I feel that I have done just about all I can do – lots
of changes. [Transition home name], new members.
Inquiries, government sending independent board to see
how they operate, also police RCMP change, etc
But I say fuck them all
Lying stupid bastard politicians
Cops, [transition home name], the whole fucking bunch
of assholes
As Krystal would say
I say when you deal with an asshole, always an asshole

July 15, 1993
Received report from RCMP in Yukon. The final report
after Larry Campbell said how [transition home name]
and RCMP had done such a good job, the report was as
I thought. No fault to officer. The Battle was long and
no one said anything without my digging and would
never say anything but all is perfect with [transition home
name] and police. What a crock of shit all lying fucks.

For nearly two years, Philip fought to receive the report written
by the lawyer on behalf of the transition home. He had determined
most of the report's information himself, but he fixated on this document as a final explanation of what went wrong. The transition
home turned down Philip's request, stating that the report's release
would breach confidentiality agreements and threaten the security
of the home's residents and staff. When Philip finally obtained a
copy through other means, they threatened to sue.

April 30, 1993
"Home owes confidentiality to every client."
A client that is in danger can not think clearly and while
you are pondering her confidentiality = you are doing
nothing for her.
The home felt it was a duty to Krystal, confidentiality of
the death.
She asked you for help – you were checking from Feb. 19/92,
which makes me wonder how much checking you did.
Ron Bax might never be caught.
Krystal confidentiality = she would want to let the law
and public know what was said and done to her
Stay here = at the home = she wanted action not just to
stay caged up.

It was December 1993, almost two years after his daughter's
death, when Philip read the lawyer's report for the first time. He
learned the name of the officer who declined Krystal an escort.

December 9, 1993
Constable Tod P – lying bastard
KILLED MY DAUGHTER

December 22, 1993
Went to Tom A—'s[1] place in the falls after work and he
gave me the check for my share of Krystal's property.
$21,000 for the property. I feel very sad because I had left
my daughter my money for when I passed away and it
does not make me happy to know that Ron Bax is still
free. Second Christmas that my daughter has missed, so
much to live for, no grandchildren – no daughter – very
sad. Love my daughter.

A few months earlier, in August, a new lead investigator replaced the initial one. In contrast to the ire Philip expresses toward most officials, he describes Constable Noack as an "honest and likeable man. My first impression – I like the man." From their first conversation in November of that year, Constable Noack helped Philip assemble an award—securing $2,000 from an RCMP fund, which would match $8,000 from Philip—and worked with *America's Most Wanted* and *Unsolved Mysteries* to feature Ronald Bax on upcoming episodes.

At the time, *Unsolved Mysteries* drew an audience of twenty-two million for every episode. According to the producer Tim Rogan, the program solved 28 percent of cases with an unknown perpetrator and 39 percent of cases with an identified fugitive.[2] As for *America's Most Wanted*, by the program's cancellation in 2012, they claimed to have helped catch 1,203 fugitives and bring home 63 missing children.

Two years after Krystal's murder, such coverage would have fuelled more tips at a moment when the case couldn't be considered "cold" but when the RCMP's supply of leads was dwindling. To move forward, they needed Colleen's approval. Constable Noack met with Colleen a few times during December 1994 and January 1995. Though she initially expressed trepidation, she did give her consent. By March 1995, however, she changed her mind. She told Constable Noack that she no longer wished to be contacted. She would not cooperate now or at any time in the future. If information was released about her, she would sue.

In the end, *Unsolved Mysteries* aired a special bulletin without Colleen's cooperation. It was short—only ninety seconds in duration, wedged between longer features. There was no re-enactment scene, and because of its nature as a special bulletin, it never aired in syndication. Still, as of January 10, 1996, the clip generated 141 calls, according to Phil's notes. One of the more promising leads concerned a sex worker in Michigan, where Bax's sister lived. (This was likely the tip Jay referred to during our early correspondence.) On December 5, 1995, a few days after the *Unsolved Mysteries* segment aired, Philip summarized a phone call with the lead investigator: "Constable Noack told me he had approx. 50 calls and one from a prostitute and he asked her what this guy was like and she told him he liked kinky sex, tied up, ex. Bax style I hear."

When Myles followed up on this detail almost thirty years later, the investigator remembered the lead and said the police had pursued it to the best of their ability. Either the lead was deemed irrelevant after the tipster was interviewed by local law enforcement, or she had omitted a name and phone number, making it difficult to contact her. The investigator couldn't remember exactly why this tip was eliminated, though it seems probable to me that the woman left her call anonymously, given the precarity of her work in relation to law enforcement.

Other calls appeared promising as well, but none panned out. The clip aired one more time in the new year.

January 19, 1996
Unsolved Mysteries to air again. Rick [Noack—the investigator] said who knows, one day we will get him.
I hope that all goes well. I told Rick in New Year we will catch Bax, that's for sure. Told Rick Paul & myself will be coming to Yukon in May 1996. I would let him know the date. I shall get tickets this week.

February 14, 1996
Time 1 PM our time. Talked to officer RCMP Whitehorse Rick Noack away for approx. 2 weeks. A great number of calls but a few very good ones but all negative. Bax still on the run. An analyst last year said

Bax had killed himself. I said this is his opinion, not mine. He agreed. Then firmly we both agreed upon – if he gets caught in our system – who knows what will happen to him. As lax as our laws seem to be, we do not know, first we must catch him then see what happens? Who knows?

Philip flew back to the Yukon in April 1996. He made dinner plans with Constable Noack for April 26, describing him as a "very good police officer as well as a gentleman." In the next entry, Philip writes that Noack is getting transferred to Alberta.

I feel crushed by this sequence every time I read it. In the first entry, we glimpse Philip preparing to meet the one person he trusts with his daughter's case. There's a current of anticipation in his writing; he's looking forward to this dinner. In the next, we realize it's a goodbye. The only person he trusts with his daughter's case is no longer working on it.

Philip would remain in touch with Noack over the coming years, calling for advice or opinions when he couldn't get through to the latest detective.

The next decade of entries resemble this one:

March 14, 1997
Called Officer in Whitehorse, left message on answering machine but no answer.

Three further officers would take over this role. With Bax still not captured by the end of his lifetime, Philip had to patch together his own attempt at resolution. His entries after 2010 read like aphorisms, written from the wisdom, or resignation, of old age.

August 8, 2010
One's life stops

One's life starts and ready to go
What this life brings no one knows
But as time goes by be it fast or slow
The mold is cast for all to know

Downfalls are often looked upon as failures. But not so,
if one takes the time to evaluate why it was not successful. Success is dedication to the goal you have chosen. The
higher the challenge the more time must be involved. To
be a success in whatever you do, you must not try and
beat time, for time will always be a winner.

[Unknown date—written on the back of a business card]
The happiest people don't have the best of everything
They just make the best of everything they have
Live simply, love generously, care deeply, speak kindly

[Unknown date]
The end is no more than the beginning
What was will always be there but always changing
One's mind must always be working
There is no end

[Unknown date]
4 things you can't recover
The stone – after it's thrown
The word – after it's thrown
The occasion – after it's missed
The time – after it's gone.

Philip Senyk died on September 20, 2019. He was eighty-two
years old.

Pursuing this case has required an excavation into old newspapers as much as anything. Although the murder and manhunt inspired a flurry of local news reports, most of them are accessible only through the labour of clicking through microfilm at the Yukon Archives. Over six years, Myles has spent around thirty hours there, sifting through thousands of articles.

What we learned is that between 1992 and 1994, Whitehorse newspapers became a spitting ground for everyone furious about Krystal's murder. In the absence of her killer, fingers speared everywhere else. The police insisted it would have been imprudent to escort Krystal from a place of safety (the transition home) to a place of potential danger (her own home). Meanwhile, the staff at the transition home felt police should have arrested Ronald Bax that night for uttering threats. Philip Senyk blamed the police for ignoring Krystal's concerns *and* the transition home for refusing to share information.

In June 1993, coroner Larry Campbell released his Judgment of Inquiry, which stated that neither the home nor the RCMP had acted improperly. Krystal had been offered a room at the home, and she chose to leave.

"Choices have to be made," Campbell told the *Star*. "My impression is Krystal Senyk was a strong-willed, independent person who was not prepared to let people push her around. People have to make choices and it may be that she was not going to allow herself to be pushed around by this type of violence."[3]

He added that he had received no trouble from the home's staff, "who do a magnificent job and work in a difficult area."[4] He didn't find anything in his investigation to merit a public inquest.[5]

On the night of the murder, a staff member left the home shortly after Krystal. As she climbed into her partner's vehicle, she spotted a man matching Bax's description skulking near the building. She thought he had something in his hands. When the staff member got home, she called the transition home to inform the staff person on shift. The *Star* reported that this person turned out the lights, lowered the blinds, and sat in the office, fearful for most of the night. When asked if the staff person's response was appropriate, Campbell replied, "I don't know. Maybe in hindsight, there should have been some calls. There is nothing to support that someone was lurking there." He suggested that people can be hypervigilant when in fearful situations—a branch of a tree may appear to be an intruder. He added that the home should allocate funds to train staff how to manage these incidents.

Of the RCMP, Campbell concluded:

> From my investigation, it was obvious that the R.C.M. Police became aware that Ms. Senyk was fearful for her safety. Further, the R.C.M. Police felt that the transition house was a safe place for Ms. Senyk. . . . Krystal Senyk asked the police officer to do a number of things that in the opinion of the police officer would not have been prudent. It is the duty of the police to protect citizens. When the citizen is in a position of safety, as was the case with Ms. Senyk, it would have been irresponsible to take her from the safety and expose her to a perceived danger. Unfortunately, there appears to have been no concrete plan on the part of the officer to follow up concerns of Ms. Senyk with an investigation.[6]

That last sentence may apply just as tragically to the weeks leading up to Krystal's murder, when her endangerment was less immediately acute, more preventable, and, infuriatingly, easier to ignore.

I can't help but think of Krystal's words on the last night of her life, spoken to a staff member at the transition home: "What needs to happen around here? Does there need to be a body before they take this seriously?"

As the investigation staggered on, both of Krystal's parents continued to navigate their bereavement. Krystal's mother, Vera, believed that Bax had left Canada and was surviving on money from his family, or on his talents as a sculptor. When Colleen withdrew her consent to participate in *Unsolved Mysteries*, Vera and Philip were devastated. The discord intensified, leading to an in-person altercation between Colleen and Vera in 1995, which had to be resolved in court. Little will be gained by belabouring the details, but what I notice in all the tumult is the human impulse to find a container for our rage, our grief, our hate. When the person responsible for violence disappears—or for whatever reason, is difficult to name—we burn whomever we can. There's a desperation here that feels deeply human: to release our grief by smearing it outward. To absolve ourselves through the purgative act of accusation. To make the deep well of our sadness more livable by transmuting it into rage.

Grief gums at the centre of this story. I've glimpsed it in Philip's notes, in the pinched words of Krystal's family. One moving monument to grief that Myles and I found was a scrapbook of condolence cards, unearthed from Jay's basement. Each page, sheathed in plastic, presents sympathy notes from friends and relatives, all of them straining for words and civility in uncivilizable circumstances. Then, at the back, the birthday cards. Philip wrote a birthday card to his daughter every year after her death.

Krystal died a month and twelve days before she would have turned thirty, and I wonder if Philip had bought the first card already. I wonder if he was getting ready to write in it when he heard the news.

30 Years Old April 13 / 92 Monday
KRYSTAL [inscribed at the centre of the card's painted iris petal]
The big 30. How time flies. I was looking at a picture of you when you were two years old and now you will never reach 30. I am 54. You are 29. I am so glad as a father that we had the love and respect for one another that we had. Few parents of broken homes do. Part of me has died with you.
Love always, Krystal.
ooo Dad ooo
xxx   xxx

In each card, Philip lists the living family members who will think of Krystal and the dead family members who will take care of her on the other side. Over the years, members from the first list join the second. He signs with a garland of *x*'s and *o*'s.

April 13 / 94 —
Dear Krystal,
    Not a day goes by that I do not think of you, hearing your laughter, seeing your smile in my mind, and always remembering how you loved your property and your home. And to think that in your home where you felt most safe – the fear is not imaginable when one knows they are going to die. And Bax with his hand revolver and you with only words. The coroner's report which I have tells me how he killed you. I am still working with Rick Noack on $10,000 reward. Going to Yukon May 14 1994 for one week and

hoping someone will see him and report to authorities but he has kept out of sight 2 years so far. Everyone in the family talks about you and our love reaches to you in God's arms.

All our lives have changed, my Mom's, Uncle P—, Aunt S—, Aunt T—, all the family never the same. Who would have known when I was a young man my daughter would be murdered.

You are always on my mind.

Love always,

Dad xxxx oooo

You would be 32 years today.

You would be 32 – me 56.

7.

THE HUNT

Vera Campbell believes her daughter was standing at her cellar door when she was shot. It's not clear whether Krystal was entering or leaving by this door: Was she facing Ronald Bax, in an altercation or an attempt to defend herself, or trying to flee? One shell casing was discharged from a high-calibre rifle. The gunshot would have left blood spatter on the wall or doorframe, helping investigators establish how close the gun was to Krystal's body, as well as the direction, angle, and trajectory of the bullet. Little of this information has been released to the public, though some sources indicate the rifle was discharged close to Krystal and that the bullet, after exiting her body, penetrated a coat closet. Both Krystal and Ron owned guns, but the one that killed Krystal was never found.

Though police found Krystal's body at 11 a.m. on March 2, they did not search Bax's property until six that evening, after the Emergency Response Team had arrived from BC. Police and civilians alike worried Bax had not finished his rampage, and sixteen individuals were taken into protective custody, including Colleen Bax and their two children. The rest of the community waited, tensely, for his capture. In the early 1990s, many Carcross residents were connected to a party line, a single telephone circuit shared by multiple households. The party line offered little privacy—you could easily listen to other people's conversations. After Krystal's murder, an RCMP officer accessed the line and warned people not to leave their homes or approach Bax if they saw him. An RCMP bulletin went out to Carcross residents about the upcoming spring break. Anyone who owned a cabin in the area was asked to inform the RCMP, specifying its location, when they planned to be there, and the number of persons in their party. They were advised to call the RCMP if they saw anything suspicious. Indeed, residents had reasons to fear each other too. As many residents hunted, many owned guns. A 1991 survey found that 67 percent of Yukon households owned at least one firearm, compared to 15 percent in Ontario.[1] The community was armed and nervous. One neighbour spotted a guy cruise by in a four-wheeler. The driver bore a faint resemblance to Bax, so the man grabbed his rifle and trained his gunsight on him until the ATV passed. Another local, a friend and artistic collaborator with Bax, waited the whole night with a rifle at his front door.

On March 3, the RCMP searched every car headed southbound on the Klondike Highway toward Skagway, Alaska, but this measure only lasted one day. The hard, crusty snow was helping the ground team cover land, but it would also facilitate Bax's escape on foot. By March 5, he had officially been charged with first-degree murder. Twenty-five to thirty officers were assigned to the case, including two members from Carcross, six from the Emergency Response Team, a helicopter pilot, and a police dog and handler, as well as uniformed and plainclothes officers in Whitehorse. As documented in an internal RCMP report dated May 1993, the initial investigation resulted in "wilderness searches, cabin/home searches, vehicle inspections, friends, neighbours and associates interviewed, medical enquiries, airline/ferry manifest inspections, international inquiries, psychological analysis and extensive distribution of wanted posters."

The first wanted posters produced little of substance, with sightings as far south as Los Angeles, as far north as Alaska, and as far east as Quebec—sometimes on the same day. (One memorable sighting was by a Constable Desjardins of Saint-Jérôme, Quebec, who thought he spotted Bax on *The Oprah Winfrey Show*.)

While the RCMP's canine unit, one dog, hunted scents from the ground, a parallel search unfolded by air.

Though the RCMP likely used their own aircraft in the days immediately following the murder, the search by helicopter with a forward-looking infrared, or FLIR, camera did not begin for another week. Again, the remote location delayed proceedings, as the FLIR camera did not arrive at the helicopter hangar until March 8. The pilot, Adam Morrison, would be flying a Bell 206B JetRanger, the camera mounted below the nose and operable by the front passenger. FLIR cameras detect any bodies warmer than the ground temperature and feed these fluorescently coded images back to the controller on a screen. The team began at Krystal's cabin, tracing grids in the area surrounding her home. Three RCMP officers flew on board with Adam: one up front operating the FLIR and two in the back, one at each window. They flew for three days, identifying many "warm bodies"—most of them animals or wood-heated cabins. They then widened their search to include the vaster territory around Carcross and Tagish Lake. Their nearest lead arrived on the morning of March 11, when the RCMP received a tip from a truck driver who thought he'd seen a light on the other side of Tutshi Lake, forty kilometres south of Carcross. At that time, that side of the lake did not contain any cabins or structures, so the light couldn't have been from someone's home.

Adam felt a wriggle of nerves as the three RCMP members boarded his helicopter that day, fully armed, in bulletproof vests. In a search not long before, the suspect had opened fire on Adam's helicopter in an attempt to shoot him down. Now on the hunt for

an armed and enraged individual—a skilled marksman, no less—
Adam didn't want to fly too low. They started at five hundred to
eight hundred feet above ground level, initially flying circles on the
other side of the lake, where the truck driver had glimpsed a light.
When they couldn't find anything from that height, Adam took
the helicopter lower. Eventually, they nosed low enough to scan
for footprints or campfire remains—but nothing looked out of the
ordinary. They continued at this level, combing the creek valley,
but no boot prints or abandoned fires were spotted. That said,
Adam remembers it had been snowing, and there were always
high winds in the area. Snow could have covered up any tracks.

As part of the investigation, a forensic psychologist formulated a
psychological profile of Bax based on interviews with his friends
and acquaintances. Dated March 4, 1992, the report describes Bax
as "a 5'7", 150 lb caucasian . . . variously engaged as an artist, sculptor, taxidermist, outfitter, woodsman, marksman, and proficient,
knowledgeable outdoorsman" with a "history of occasional cocaine
and/or alcohol use/abuse." The report offered the following points
for the investigators' consideration:

1. This suspect is extremely dangerous:
a) He has already killed in apparent cold blood;
b) He knows that his victim is dead;
c) He believes he has little to lose at this time;
d) He is well-armed and a skilled shooter;
e) His normal "inhibitors" to aggression are likely low or
non-existent immediately after the first shooting

2. This suspect if cornered, will shoot, suicide or both:
a) [withheld by RCMP];

b) The current manhunt will trigger his "survival instinct," moving his frame of mind from "I've done something terrible" to "I'm now just trying to survive" to "it's me or them" or "I'm going to die anyways";
c) Under extreme stress, he is "wired" and far more likely to use lethal force;
d) He may want to die at the hands of someone else, and to accomplish this he will provoke fire by shooting first

3. This suspect will not respect RCMP officers:
a) He has a known dislike for Police;
b) He believes Police to be on "her side," meaning that of the wife and/or victim;
c) Police Officers will become the focal point for all of his pent-up anger and frustration

4. This suspect may do unpredictable things:
a) He is entirely capable of an ambush or trap;
b) Under extreme pressure, his thinking may not be logical or predictable.

Subsequent analyses (including one in 1995, judging from Philip's notes) have indicated that Bax likely killed himself immediately after the murder. In those first days, however, the police treated him as very possibly alive.

By the end of March 1992, the investigation had cost the RCMP over $80,000 and 1,800 overtime hours had been logged, on top of 1,400 regular hours and 250 hours by "guards and matrons" hired to perform support duties and clerical work. Approximately $20,000 went toward car rentals, feeding the individuals in protective custody, and chartering the FLIR helicopter.[2]

The internal report from 1993, based on a case analysis

conducted by Corporal Roberts of RCMP's "K" Division (Alberta) the previous year, states that "after examining numerous homicide files throughout Alberta, British Columbia, Saskatchewan and the United States, I found this file to be one of the most comprehensively investigated files I have examined."

By March 13, the "manhunt" was downsized to a more typical investigation, involving the two Carcross members and several plainclothes officers from Whitehorse, who continued to pursue tips and leads.[3] At this time, the police announced their three theories:

1. Bax hiked into the bush and killed himself.
2. Bax hiked into the bush to hide.
3. Bax fled the area entirely.

To this day, the RCMP maintains that there is a 70 percent chance Bax committed suicide immediately after murdering Krystal. Several facts support this theory. For one, he'd threatened more than once to kill himself, often to deter his wife from leaving him. He was known to have extreme mood swings, and was described by a close friend as "despondent." He threatened to kill himself a few weeks before the murder, which would have been around the first time Colleen moved into the transition home. A friend once witnessed Bax pointing a gun to his head. This friend tried to grab it from him; a struggle ensued. The friend let go, concerned the trigger would be clenched by accident. Bax refused to release the gun, but he did not proceed with an attempt.

Further facts to support the suicide theory include Bax's killing his dog Kato shortly before the murder because he "couldn't stand to see his dog on a chain." The implication is that if Bax planned to kill himself, he wanted to shoot his dog first, so the animal wouldn't end up in a shelter. (The same theory might hold, however, if Bax planned to murder someone and leave town.) Another detail that supports the suicide theory is that at the time of the murder, Bax was apparently broke. His truck, wallet, ID, and outdoor gear, as well as a paper that could be construed as a suicide note, were found at his home. Myles and I both raised eyebrows at this possible suicide note, but so far the RCMP has not released a copy. Police did acknowledge at the time that some of Bax's outdoor gear was missing. At the time of writing, thirty years have passed since Bax's disappearance, and no body or firearm has been found.

In the 1993 report, Corporal Roberts concludes that "in all likelihood, Ronald Bax committed suicide shortly after killing Krystal Senyk. . . . Very few recommendations can be made in this file. In their attempts to prove that a. Ronald Bax was responsible for the death of Krystal Senyk and b. attempting to locate Ronald Bax, the investigators have covered most aspects of the investigation."

In our copy, sent directly from the Whitehorse Detachment General Investigation Section, the word "most" is underlined in ballpoint pen.

The second theory proposed by the RCMP in March 1992—that Bax disappeared into the bush and remained in hiding—is supported by Bax's skill in the outdoors. He worked as a big game guide, which involved hiking into the mountains in search of Dall sheep and grizzly, sighting animals for tourists to hunt as trophies. He knew the land surrounding Whitehorse and Carcross extremely well, and was described by a former roommate, another outdoorsman, as "second to none" in the bush. Though a bulletin had been issued across Canada and Alaska, and the border crossings had been on alert since Krystal's body was discovered on March 2, Bax had a significant lead. Witnesses indicate that Krystal left the transition home around 9:30 p.m. on March 1. Her friend Suzanne told Philip Senyk that Krystal dropped by her house that evening and left by 10:45. Philip recorded in his diary that it would take approximately fifty minutes for her to drive home to Carcross, which suggests Krystal was killed between 11:30 p.m. and midnight on March 1. Corporal Roberts's report confirms that timing: "judging by the way Krystal was dressed and the amount of snow on the BAX vehicles, he probably killed her prior to midnight March 1, 1992."

Krystal's body wasn't discovered by police for another eleven to twelve hours, giving Bax plenty of time to hike into the surrounding mountains and scrubland. As one friend worded it: "[The police] were all terrified of him. They had his house circled around—helicopters—it wasn't until the next day they flash-banged and kicked his door down. They were babysitting an empty house the whole time. How much of a lead do you want to give this guy? He could have walked to Fraser by then."

Bax had every skill and resource to live off the land. His friend continued: "It was—what was that, mid-winter? From Ron's place, his house, you could look down and there's a confluence of that little river in Carcross. There's always an open section of water out there. I told the RCMP, if he didn't shoot himself, he could have just walked into the water there. They wasted so much time—there were snow flurries. They wasted so much time that they fucked themselves. They were flying around with the FLIR . . . they saw a moose, but they didn't see Ron. By that time, he could have been crawled under a rock or gone in the wind. In an area that he knew very well . . . It was so mishandled."

As many locals have remarked over the course of the investigation: the Yukon is an easy place to disappear.

As years pass, it grows likelier that the second and third theories have merged. If Bax had been hiding in the wilderness for a period, he's likely fled the area by now too. Carcross is en route to the US border. Krystal's cabin on Crag Lake is a ninety-minute drive to Skagway, the nearest American city, and Bax had eleven hours before alerts would have been distributed. While the long-term population of Skagway is tiny (692 residents were reported in the 1990 census), every day in the summer season, cruise ships bring thousands of tourists, making it easier to slip into obscurity. March would be too early for cruise season, but it's notable that a record three hundred thousand visitors were reported in Skagway in 1992 as they celebrated the fiftieth anniversary of the Alaska Highway.

It was easier to cross the border in the early 1990s, especially a remote northern one. One former RCMP officer, who served in Whitehorse at the time of the murder, remembers that border guards rarely noted down licence numbers, never mind checked passports. At night, the border wasn't always manned. The officer had known Krystal as a resident of the community and the only woman in his shotgun club. He was not directly involved in the investigation, but it unfolded around him at the station, and he paid attention. He says it would have been very easy to catch a ride across the border, then "flip around," that is, change one's appearance. Indeed, fifty-tonne tractor-trailers used to route past Carcross twenty-four hours a day carrying ore from the Faro mine to Skagway. If anyone could hop one of those trucks and avoid freezing to death, it would be Bax, according to friends. If he shaved his moustache and darkened his hair, his appearance would be radically different.

On March 30, 1992, the *Whitehorse Star* reported that the RCMP had questioned a second suspect: Bax's best friend, Nick Cannell, who may have helped him escape in his pickup.[4] However, soon after this rumour circulated, Cannell was cleared as a person of interest: he had a convincing alibi and passed a polygraph test.

A woman who used to work at the transition home remembers a conversation with a hairdresser friend who knew a group of "rough biker dudes" living by Kookatsoon Lake, between Whitehorse and Carcross. The woman described these guys as "real heavy-duty misogynists." After Krystal's murder, the friend told her Krystal "was trying to get in between [Ron] and his wife. Those guys from Kookatsoon were ready to help him because they didn't like that."

"She all but said they were the ones who helped him get out of there," the woman told Myles over the phone. At the time, she had been good friends with Colleen's brother, who told her, "Oh no, he'd never kill himself. He's gonna get away." Apparently, Colleen told her brother the same thing.

If Bax is alive, he could be anywhere, not necessarily in North America. He had a good "Spanish friend" he'd met at a trade show in the United States who was something of an artistic mentor. Shortly before Krystal's murder, Ron received a parcel in the mail from an address in Spain. The size and weight were consistent with a gun, by Colleen's judgment. She never opened the package, but she later told one of the lead investigators that she wondered if it had contained the murder weapon.

8.

TRAIL
OR
NO
TRAIL

Residents of Whitehorse and Carcross continue to swap myths and musings about Bax's escape. As Bax lived near the Carcross Airport, some speculate he flew over the border into Alaska in a small aircraft like an ultralight or Cessna, which a friend may have owned or had access to. According to the pilot Adam Morrison, who had helped search for Bax after the murder, ultralights are nimble enough to take off from any stretch of even ground, not just official runways. They can stay in the air for up to ninety minutes, and it would have taken no more than forty-five minutes to cross the border. An ultralight is also quiet, except for the noise it produces on takeoff. However, you can't fly a single-engine aircraft such as an ultralight or Cessna in the dark.

That time of year, Bax wouldn't have been able to get off the ground until eight or so in the morning, shaving a good eight hours off his getaway time. While some foolhardy pilots may attempt to leave earlier than official daylight times posted by air stations, it would be dangerous—not least because Carcross is surrounded by hills and mountains. *Foolhardy* is an adjective that could describe Bax, but he'd have to find a willing pilot who (1) knew the area intimately and (2) was just as reckless. The RCMP looked into the flight theory—they even discussed it on the FLIR-equipped helicopter as they searched for his tracks—but some have wondered if they should have pursued it more closely. According to Krystal's brother, Gord, several people in the area heard an unscheduled flight take off, though presumably these reports didn't hold up to police questioning.

As a wilderness guide who took wealthy businessmen into the bush to hunt, Bax did know pilots. There were hundreds of pilots operating out of Carcross and Whitehorse in the early nineties, according to Adam Morrison. Many flew into Carcross for fuel, scenic tours, lunch, or training. The main difference between flying out of remote communities and flying from a major metropolis is that there's no requirement to file an official flight plan with Transport Canada. Anyone who flies locally out of small communities could use a "company flight note," which means you just tell someone what time you're leaving, where you're going, and when you'll return. Most times, Adam flew on a flight plan with Transport Canada, which included departure time, destination, time en route, return time, and the number of "souls" on board. He would only rarely use a company note. However, private pilots, or people who owned their own planes, could leave communities without filing notes of any kind. It wouldn't be smart or recommended, but no one would know.

RCMP checked the Skagway airport to see if a plane had landed there and found nothing, though the airport likely would not have been staffed before official daylight time. Notably, many airstrips in the Yukon and Alaska are not published or officially regulated. Some of them are even built by hand by big game outfitters. Adam himself had helped construct a few of them. "An undetected landing would be easy to accomplish," he said. "As an outfitter guide, Bax would know of these strips."

The main stumbling block in this theory is the timing. If Bax did depart in the dim early light, with a reckless pilot he befriended in the bar or on one of his wilderness treks, it would have been easy to land somewhere remote and hike into obscurity. However, Bax had every skill to hike straight from Carcross. Why use a loud, obvious form of transit when you could disappear without a murmur? Unless you were trying to avoid leaving tracks in the snow. But then, why not catch a ride the old-fashioned way? Indeed, the Klondike Highway, which connects Carcross and Skagway, directly passes Tutshi Lake, where the truck driver had reported seeing a light.

Another rumour in particular always intrigued me. In the summer of 2008, a Whitehorse resident received a phone call from her brother Bob in Ontario. He had been staying at a secluded campground off Lake Huron in Ontario, next to the Michigan border. He met a man who was waiting at the campground for his visa so that he could cross the border. This man was with a woman who had family in Michigan, and they had access to a house in Florida. Ronald Bax has a sister who lives in Michigan, and many have wondered whether she has helped him financially, though this rumour remains unsubstantiated. She denies that she has heard from him, suggesting their relationship was never close. The mysterious man at the campground, who went by the name of Henry, was Canadian—a "woodsman"—and he played guitar. He, Bob, and John from the neighbouring trailer shared a few evenings around the campfire, drinking beer and singing old songs that Bob recognized from the Yukon. Bob asked Henry how he knew those songs and discovered he used to live in the Yukon. Henry had recalled "a small town with a *C* next to Whitehorse," which could only be Carcross. He knew all about the territory and proceeded to boast about his bush skill—how he'd helped someone escape the Yukon after a "bad situation" in the early nineties. Bob asked how useful bush skills were nowadays, and Henry said, "They're useful when people want to disappear."

The moment Bob mentioned that his sister lived in Whitehorse, Henry clammed up. He had been staying at the campground for a month, but he and the woman ("Linda") left within a week of this conversation. Bob remembers Henry was keeping a pile of sticks, which struck him as unusual, as the wood was green—you couldn't burn it. He was carving walking sticks and selling them for ten dollars apiece. He also crafted violins, he said, for a girl "down east" in the Maritimes. One reason Henry was having difficulty crossing the border was that he couldn't provide an address. "This is home right here," he had said, pointing to the camper on the back of his pickup truck.

He and Linda both played guitar skilfully; they played in the campground church service. Bob and John both described the man as tall—at least six feet—and around seventy years old at the time. The Whitehorse resident reported this tip to the RCMP in 2012, four years after Henry and Linda passed through the campground. While Constable Thur, the lead investigator at the time, never suspected Henry could be Ronald Bax, he wondered if this man had helped Bax to disappear. According to John, the girlfriend lived across the border in Michigan but visited Henry at the Canadian campground on weekends. Constable Thur asked John and his wife if they could obtain a name from the campground records. They tried that Victoria Day weekend, but the campground withheld the information, citing privacy concerns. Constable Thur followed up on his own, but the campground couldn't find anyone in the logbook under the names Henry or Linda. It was another year before Thur asked the Sarnia RCMP to peruse the records themselves. They did so in August 2013, but reached the same conclusion: there were no records in the relevant time frame that provided information about Henry or Linda, nor any clients who listed an American address.

In 2018, John told me that Henry had returned to the campground seven or eight years after his first appearance. Henry had tried to find John, but John had moved campsites. To my knowledge, they never made contact again. While this remains a possibly significant tip, no further information has come from it.

Many have speculated that Bax crossed the Yukon border by foot over one of the surrounding mountains. Carcross and Skagway are linked by the Chilkoot Trail, a famous route trekked by miners during the Klondike gold rush. Today, hikers still backpack this trail, which takes three to five days to complete, depending on one's fitness level. From Skagway, ferries run to other Alaskan cities such as Haines and Juneau, as well as south to Bellingham, Washington. It was easy to hop ferries in the early nineties. One officer at the time used to investigate major theft, and he said several perpetrators escaped this way—by walking onto boats without attracting the staff's attention.

In March 1992, a Fairbanks police blotter reported that an individual thought he had spotted Bax at the Skagway ferry terminal. When police from Haines investigated the lead, however, they only discovered a tourist from the lower states.

The officer who worked in Whitehorse at the time of Krystal's murder remembers RCMP waiting for the Emergency Response Team to arrive from BC. "That would have been very time-consuming," he said to me over the phone. "It extended the time. Do you follow what I mean by that?"

Like Morrison, he recalled a light snowfall. Data compiled by Environment Canada confirms that one centimetre fell on March 2—not a lot, but forty-one centimetres lay on the ground already. Temperatures dropped to a low of minus eighteen by March 3, forming a crust that would make it harder for the police dog to follow scents.

A former roommate of Ronald Bax described him as "an animal" out there in the wilderness. He could hike across a border, trail or no trail. When we asked what he thought of the RCMP's theories, he shook his head. "There's no way he killed himself. Not a chance in hell." Bax was too proud, the roommate said. When RCMP questioned him in the weeks following Krystal's murder, he warned them: "He's going to disappear."

In March 2015, an article was published in the *Press Register* of Clarksdale, Mississippi, about a man wanted by the Canadian police who might be living in the nearby town of Rena Lara. A woman in Rena Lara had submitted a tip to CrimeStoppers after her husband let the man move into their home. The lodger had introduced himself as Clinton Hill,[1] but she found an information card with another identity on it: Ronald Jeffrey Bax. She didn't recognize this name and typed it into Google, discovering the RCMP wanted listing. The Coahoma County Sheriff's Office detained Clinton Hill for questioning, but when his fingerprints did not match those on file for Ronald Bax (taken in Ontario in 1983), they released him. According to the *Press Register*, Clinton had supplied drugs to residents in Rena Lara, and that's why locals hadn't turned him in. He looked the same as in Bax's photos online, according to the article, "with a little more gray hair and a short beard."[2] The article also suggests that the man in question had suffered serious burns on his hands, though this detail was not mentioned by the Sheriff's Office. In a phone interview with ABC News, Sheriff Charles Jones stated:

> We made contact with this individual. He didn't have any ID. Any form of identification. We couldn't ID the individual. We took this individual in for questioning at the Coahoma County Sheriff's Office. Once we got there, we fingerprinted the subject. We went on the national database to send the prints back. It was discovered that this guy was not Ronald Bax.

During our research, a woman contacted Myles through his website. She had been hanging out with a friend when she noticed the wanted photo of Ronald Bax on her friend's basement fridge. The image, printed from the internet, was next to a photo of a rosy young man holding a baby. This same young man was in another photo, raising a beer to the photographer, his arm around a familiar blond guy in a plaid shirt: Ronald Bax. After a few emails back and forth, the woman called Myles and said: "I'm at Ronnie Bax's house."

Myles's face blanched, as did mine when he told me later. Turns out, Ronald Bax had a cousin in Ontario who was also named Ronald Bax and went by Ronnie for short. At our request, the woman asked after his wanted cousin's whereabouts, but Ronnie didn't say much. When asked whether he could be in Mississippi, Ronnie scoffed: "If anything, he'd be in Florida." She asked why Florida. He changed the subject.

Naturally, the Mississippi lead caught the attention of Const. Craig Thur in 2015. He spoke to the informant over the phone, and the FBI conducted their own analysis of the fingerprints. The

FBI drew the same conclusion as the county sheriff: the prints didn't match.

The reporter who wrote the initial article had worked at the paper for three years as an editor and crime reporter. Rena Lara's population is tiny and it is geographically isolated by a levee, she explained to me over the phone. Though nearby Clarksdale has more income flow thanks to blues tourism, the Coahoma County Sheriff's Office is "outdated" and "deteriorating." As recently as 2015, when the reporter left the area, they still kept handwritten rather than digitized records. She described the county sheriff himself as "notoriously incompetent." I asked for an example, and she said the *Press Register* collaborated with the sheriff to publish the arrests every week. Once, he sent over a handwritten record for first-degree murder, which the paper published—only to hear from the accused's outraged family. The sheriff's office had made a mistake: the arrest was for theft, not murder. The reporter suggested that incidents like this were not uncommon. In the three years she followed local CrimeStoppers meetings, the representative for the sheriff's office had gone just once, compared with an officer with the Clarksdale Police Department, who attended every meeting.

Constable Thur acknowledged the Mississippi informant's reasons to suspect her lodger's identity. The man spoke with a northern accent, had expressed an interest in taxidermy and sculpture, and didn't possess proper ID. (The informant believes he destroyed the ID with the name Ronald Bax on it.)

The informant worked as a manual labourer and was no stranger to gnarled fingers, the reporter told me, but she'd emphasized the lodger's hands were "really messed up." The *Press Register* article specifies the individual had "suffered serious burns on his hands."

Constable Thur requested a copy of the FBI fingerprint comparison, as well as photographs of Clinton Hill. He told Myles over email:

> When I received the photographs and fingerprint report
> I was able to confirm that although Terry Clinton HILL
> did have a resemblance to Ronald BAX, his fingerprints
> were significantly different. I have the Federal Bureau
> of Investigation report prepared in Clarksburg West
> Virginia on Tuesday, March 10th, 2015 documenting
> that an FBI analyst had completed a manual comparison
> of the fingerprints of Terry Clinton HILL and Ronald
> Jeffrey BAX and concluded that the fingerprints were of
> two different individuals.

Presumably, the report would have noted if the fingerprints indicated signs of mutilated prints, as in the case of burned hands. In subsequent correspondence, Constable Thur confirms:

> In your e-mail from August 13th, 2018 you stated that
> Terry Clinton HILL had "serious burns on his hands."
> I obtained a copy of the fingerprints of Terry Clinton
> HILL taken in Clarksdale Mississippi on Monday,
> March 9th, 2015. I saw no evidence of any serious burns
> on HILL's fingers. The fingerprints were suitable for
> manual comparison with the fingerprints of Ronald BAX
> and they were clearly the fingerprints of a different individual.

His judgment is conclusive, but given the accumulation of other similarities, and the fuzzy detail around Hill's hands, this lead continued to give me pause. As for Clinton Hill, the reporter told me he disappeared soon after his release. Later, I would learn that while he did leave the county, without saying goodbye to the man who housed him for two years, his exit was not so immediate or succinct.

If fingerprints were the main evidence that proved Clinton Hill was not Ronald Bax, I wanted to understand more about them. I knew that no two individuals possessed the same fingerprints, not even identical twins with the same DNA. Left alone, they remain unchanged through a person's lifetime; as new skin cells form, they recreate the same ridges and furrows. But what if you don't leave them alone?

In February 2019, I spoke with the lawyer who was named as the recipient of the report written by the transition home's advocate in 1992. We were discussing Krystal's case when I mentioned the information card that allegedly surfaced in Mississippi four years earlier.

She replied, rather casually, that she used to work as a criminal defence lawyer in Vancouver, which involved a number of drug cases. Plastic surgeons can alter fingerprints, she told me, suggesting this practice was not uncommon. In a later email exchange, she repeated this detail: clients she knew in those days used to visit a plastic surgeon in Vancouver or LA to get their prints altered.

"They used to have their nails removed," she told me, "and then my understanding is that the surgeon would somehow tighten/ loosen the skin under the nail, and it would affect the print."

Altered fingerprints fall into three categories: destruction, deformation, and imitation. To destroy fingerprints, individuals abrade, wound, burn, or apply chemicals to their fingertips—all of which can be detected by today's quality control software (and by the FBI's manual analysis). With fingerprint deformation, a surgeon twists the friction ridge into abnormal edge patterns. Portions of the skin are removed and the edges joined in different positions. It has been suggested that distorted prints may pass undetected by quality control software, as deformations don't reduce the quality of the image. In the final category, fingerprint imitation, surgeons transplant friction ridge skin from other fingers, palms, toes, and soles onto the finger to appear as a natural fingerprint pattern. The central region of the original print is replaced with the central region of a different piece of skin. It's hard to assess how successful this type of print alteration can be. Presumably, successful imitations pass undetected.

When it comes to mutilating your fingerprints, there is a spectrum of sophistication—from gnawing your own fingers in the back of a squad car to plastic surgery that costs tens of thousands of dollars—with an equal spectrum of results. In January 2019, a month before my conversation with the former defence lawyer, a drug trafficker was caught after having evaded police for fifteen years by cutting and burning his fingerprints, then replacing them with micro-implants. According to Spanish police, the suspect had used "very sophisticated methods to alter the fingerprints of both hands so that he couldn't be identified. He used skin implants to change the shape of his prints so that the scars beneath couldn't be detected."

People have surgically altered their fingerprints to cross borders as well, as in the case of Lin Rong, a twenty-seven-year-old woman who paid $15,000 to have her fingerprints swapped between her right and left hands. She then entered Japan with a fake passport and remained in the country illegally. Her identity was not detected when her finger and thumb were scanned at the Japanese border. Rong was arrested only later, when caught counterfeiting a marriage licence.

Despite the conclusions of RCMP and the Coahoma County Sheriff's Office, I could not lightly let this tip go. How is it that someone in Mississippi had stumbled on an information card in the name of Ronald Bax, or at the very least, knew his name? While a fugitive probably wouldn't carry belongings that could betray their identity, is it possible that Bax had held on to something for sentimental reasons? A business card for his sculpture business, for example? If there was a chance that Bax had fled to the US under the relative security of altered prints, I wanted to find out.

9.

RENA
LARA

It was 11 a.m., early for lunch, and only a few others joined us at the Great River Country Store in Rena Lara, Mississippi. My friend Jasmine and I sat at a table for an hour while I scratched down notes, and she snapped the odd, furtive photo. The men at the next table wore hunting vests and cowboy hats. It looked like a hunting lodge in there. I counted at least eight taxidermied buck heads, and even the fridge was backed with glossy camouflage. I was thinking: the taxidermy, the hunters—if Bax did pass through here, he would have felt at home.

I was admiring a clock on the wall—collaged, impressively, with bald eagles *and* crucifixes—when a man at another table greeted us with a warm "Y'all aren't from around here, are you." He was here with his children and their grandmother. His name was Ricky. He had blond-grey hair, pliant eyes, a blue check shirt. He had lived in Rena Lara his whole life, he told us. We chatted over the remains of our food, though I didn't ask the questions I really wanted to, like: Did you hear of a Canadian guy who passed through town five years ago? Locals had told me that Rena Lara's population was two hundred, "most of them kin." I didn't know who I was talking to yet.

Ever since my phone conversation with the *Press Register*

journalist in 2018, I'd known I had to come here. What if it *had* been Bax in Rena Lara? After decades without a trace, did he graze so close to capture? It was a thought that kept me up at night— rereading the *Press Register* article, clicking through Rena Lara on Google Earth, searching the individuals named in the article for kernels of information. I couldn't let this thread, or my obses- sive mind-tracking, rest until I travelled down there and spoke to whomever I could.

Myles couldn't come because of work and life obligations, and for a while, that stumped me. I didn't feel safe knocking on strangers' doors on my own. Not in Mississippi, where, fairly or not, I assumed most people were armed, and I'd be poking around about a possible murderer. In the end I asked Jasmine, the friend who was with me when I began seriously pursuing this research again in 2018. As long-distance friends (we met at a retreat in Colorado in 2017), our meet-ups always involved travel. And Mississippi wasn't so far from Texas, where she was from.

We arrived in November 2019, spending a week in Memphis, then a few days at an Airbnb in Clarksdale, a small city twenty-four kilometres east of Rena Lara. I hoped to speak with four people: Sheriff Charles Jones; coroner and funeral director Walt Madison; the Rena Lara resident who had housed Clinton Hill, Doug Cussen; and Doug's former wife, Sandy, who'd found the information card and dialed CrimeStoppers.[1] Realistically, I thought the Sheriff and coroner would be unwilling to talk, while Doug and Sandy would be difficult to locate, and if I found them, also unwilling to talk. Worst-case scenario, I'd record setting details, I told myself.

If left to my own devices, that might have been all I got. Jasmine runs a bar with her partner in Houston, and she advised me that the fastest way to know a town is through their bartenders—espe- cially if you leave a "fat tip." This strategy would inform our search over the coming days, starting that night, when a bartender in

Clarksdale pointed us to a friend, Riley, who lived in Rena Lara. Riley worked at a place around the corner, but couldn't talk that night, as it was a full house. We tipped her 60 percent and said we'd return the next day.

That night, at our Airbnb, we were settling in for the evening when my bedside lamp started to turn on and off. I don't mean the bulb ambiguously flickered. It turned off. Then it turned on. Then it turned off. This was accompanied by even thumps of a switch in the breaker room. As Jasmine and I watched—amused, if disconcerted, by the light show—the thumping accelerated, and with it, the flickering of light: on—off—on—off—on—off-on-off-on-offonoff, as if someone was standing at the breaker box, shunting the switch back and forth. Then the light in the back room began to flick—at the same steadily revving rate as the bedside lamp—while every other light in the apartment remained stable. At this point, I thought either a ghost would introduce herself from the masonry, or a fuse would blow, or we'd perish in an electrical fire. So we unplugged the lamp. The sound of the switch continued, but at this point, it was too late to call an electrician or the Airbnb host. I still felt on edge, but I was too exhausted to think of another solution. I inserted earplugs and fell asleep.

The next morning, our power was out. Our Airbnb host called the utilities company. As Jasmine and I dressed, six men in orange jumpsuits arrived. They seemed, at that moment, like overkill. When I explained what happened, one said: "Sounds like ghosts."

I showed them the videos on my phone.

"Yup," the same electrician said, stretching out the vowel. "Ghosts."

I laughed at the joke, but after a few minutes, they noticed one of their crew had elected to wait outside.

We would continue to see these men every day of our trip, working on the power line up the street. Each morning they asked if the situation had resolved itself (it did for one day, then we lost power again, including hot water). We would say no, and one would reply: "What y'all need down yonder's a haint tree."

I had to look that up. A haint tree is a post decked with glass bottles, to ward off haints, or wandering spirits.

The funeral home was plush and white, with a decadent stuffiness that befitted a funeral parlour. I proceeded to the office with the most polite and daughterly comportment I could muster. Four white men stood around a desk. All of the men were large; all of them wore suits.

"Hi," I said. "I'm looking for Walt Madison."

One stepped forward. He looked to be in his fifties, with cramped eyes and generous cheeks. "I'm he."

The journalist had told me over the phone that Walt might be willing to talk. He hadn't wanted his name in the paper at the time, but he knew of the man who'd lived with Doug. I emailed Mr. Madison in the month before my trip to see if he would meet me, but I never heard from him. I didn't expect this conversation to go very far.

"My name's Eliza," I said. "I emailed you about a former resident of Rena Lara."

"Oh right," he said.

"Do you have a few minutes to talk?"

To my surprise, he showed us into his boardroom. His son-in-law, Cameron, joined too.

Walt remembered the incident: Sheriff Jones had detained a resident of Rena Lara for two days because an information card connected him with a Canadian homicide. He didn't know the man personally, but he knew Doug and Sandy. He said Sandy had "turned her life around" after she left Doug. She worked in the area as a handyperson. "She'd probably talk to you," he said. "I can give you her phone number."

When I mused aloud whether Sandy would be alarmed to receive a phone call about this, Walt shook his head.

"Sandy's tough," he said. "She's a good Christian, and she's tough."

By contrast, he described Doug as "a scam artist alcoholic." Doug worked as a carpenter, he said. He once charged Walt $1,800 for a job he never completed. He did the same for another local, except he charged $5,000 up front, and again never finished the work. When I asked for a physical description of Doug, Cameron mentioned he always wore a white T-shirt.

Walt nodded in agreement. "He has a limp handshake," he added.

I asked if it would be unsafe for Jasmine and me to knock on Doug's door. Walt said no. Doug was harmless, he said—just down-and-out. His mother died the month before, he told us. Now Doug was living in her house—sixth on the right once you enter Rena Lara, next to a "ring of tricycles" that his mother used to collect.

Out of all the people we would speak to in Rena Lara, including Doug's friends and neighbours, only Walt knew Doug's mother had passed. I found this odd for such a small town. Despite the animosity between him and Doug, Walt buried his mother for free, "because it was the right thing to do." It occurred to me that in an area of this size, the funeral director, more than the preachers, more than the police, more than the bar staff, would know everyone.

As I clarified directions to Doug's house, Walt said: "Listen, I'm delivering a funeral in ten minutes. Why don't you come back here for two? I'll drive you to Rena Lara myself."

That afternoon, I rode with Walt and Cameron while Jasmine followed in our rented Jeep.

"This was our main store district," Walt mentioned, as we drove out of town. "Before Walmart came in, Christmas time, it was so busy they had police in the middle of the street so you could back out." The population had been thirty-five to forty thousand while he was growing up, but it had declined to seventeen. I asked why. "People move to find better education," he said. "Look at it this way. Mississippi is the last in the country for education. Coahoma County is the last in Mississippi. So we're the last in the nation."

We crossed a bridge, and the brick Colonials and weedy parking lots faded into a poplar-lined street with two cars in every driveway. If not quite "plantation," the mansions appeared aspiringly antebellum in design, with Greek Revival columns and rangy verandas. Over the course of the twenty-five-minute drive, Cameron, in the front passenger seat, attempted to find a photograph of Doug on Facebook.

"His vehicle is black," Cameron said. "Not white. I remember now. A Chevy."

"You're still searching for photos over there?" I said.

"I know I've seen one."

We turned onto a country highway that cut through ploughed cotton fields. I asked Walt how well he knew Doug.

"I knew his mother forty years," he said. "He's got two sisters. Shelly and Veronica. Shelly's got snakes in her head. She's nuts. Dopehead."

"She uses drugs?"

"Yes. Crystal meth."

We turned onto a wooded road, which led past a pecan farm and into Rena Lara.

"Lots of deer out here," Walt said. "That's where that guy would like to be. Lots of hunting. People like him poach. Wild hogs, turkey, deer," he listed. "Doves. Squirrels."

That guy, I realized, meant Clinton Hill or Ronald Bax.

"That's Doug," Cameron said, passing me his phone. "Except he's skinnier now. Due to the drinking."

This man looked average-sized. I couldn't imagine him skinnier. He wore the white T-shirt they'd mentioned.

"Was he living with Sandy behind the levee?" Walt asked his son-in-law. Cameron couldn't remember.

Rena Lara is cinched around the highway, and we'd been driving on this highway for some time. Once the clapboard prefabs and trailers started lining the road, we were there. Cameron began counting them aloud.

"One, two, three, four, five . . . Yep, we were right. It's the sixth one."

"That's it?" I said. I certainly would have missed the rusted tricycles tucked behind a bracket of pine trees.

"That's it," Walt said. He offered to show me where Doug's father lived, for good measure. We drove on: past the Country Store, past the Baptist church. Cameron pointed out Doug's truck in his dad's driveway.

"Maybe he's here," I said.

"Maybe," said Cameron. "But I noticed Doug's front door was open. The truck belongs to his dad. Maybe he took it back."

Cameron didn't say much, but he didn't miss much either.

We drove past Doug's father's house and turned onto the road that led back to the highway. Here, Walt pulled over.

"Y'all let people know where you are if you get out and knock on somebody's door," he said.

"We will," I said, though the thought hadn't occurred to me.

"Two young ladies . . . ," he said.

"Don't worry," I said. "We'll let someone know."

"It can get dangerous," he continued. "Two ladies walking up to someone's door."

His repetition of this point made me shift in my seat. "Do you think . . . we shouldn't knock on Doug's door?"

"Oh, he isn't going to bother you none. Like I say, he's wimpy. I just think you need to call somebody and say, hey we're at 4375 Highway 1 and we'll check back in when we're in the car."

"Yes," I agreed. "That's sensible."

Behind us, Jasmine pulled up in the Jeep.

"Would you describe . . . ," I began. "Doug. Is he smart? He got away with those scams."

"He talks a good game," Walt replied. "What he did at my house was good work. He found a water leak at the funeral home we've been looking for for years. That's why I trusted him when he said, 'I had this happen and this happen, can you advance my money.' Then he didn't finish the job."

"Right," I said.

"I really wouldn't mention my name," Walt said.

"Of course—"

"I don't care, but you'd get more out of him if you don't."

"Okay," I said. "Good to know."

"Now, uh, you text somebody and let 'em know where you're getting out at. If you want, text me. I don't have my phone right this minute, but you text me when you get in and you text me when you leave."

I was promising to do so when Jasmine opened the passenger door and thrust her phone toward my face.

"It's the sheriff," she said.

We had been trying to reach Sheriff Charles Jones for days. I didn't think he'd call us back. I thanked Walt and Cameron for their help and hopped out of their SUV.

"Sorry to keep you waiting," I said, conscious of the delay as I fumbled Jasmine's phone onto speaker. Then, as if by explanation: "We were just with Walt Madison."

The line remained quiet. I asked if he saw my email inquiry, which had been forwarded to the communications officer.

"Yes," Jones said. "All we can tell you is what we know. That is, we followed up on a lead. And it didn't, it didn't turn out to be the right guy. We kept the guy on and—that's all I can tell you. We followed up on the lead and the guy, the guy was not the guy y'all are looking for."

"Right. I understand that," I said as I climbed into the Jeep. "Especially as his fingerprints didn't match. Is that correct?"

"Some other things also. Besides his fingerprints. He wasn't the right guy."

I wanted to know what those "other things" were, but people seemed to be less guarded in person. I asked if we could meet so I could ask a few questions.

"I don't know any other details," the sheriff said. "All I can tell you is we were following up on a case. I would never come into something I have no facts on."

"Do you recall a physical description?"

"I wasn't the one that went out. It was— I'm sure we kept a picture of the guy. But it's been so long ago. Four, five years ago. I don't know."

"You're not sure where we might find that photo?"

"No, not at this point. When we got the information that it wasn't the right guy, we didn't have any reason to keep on the case. To keep it up."

"Wouldn't you archive the paperwork?"

"I don't know. I can't confirm that right now, because of the fact it wasn't the right guy. Any time we have a person of interest and it doesn't turn out to be the right guy, we don't do anything else with it."

"Do you know who initially arrested him or took him in for fingerprinting?"

"I can't remember."

We fell into a mutually uncomfortable silence.

"Okay," I said. "Well, I appreciate you calling us back."

"If I can get some more information, I'll let you know. I'll look into it if I can get a minute."

"Thank you," I said. "Do you know anyone else who might have more information?"

"Not at this point, no. Not right now. We have so many cases. And tell me—you're just a writer. You're just doing a book."

"That's correct, yes."

"So in Canada—who in Canada do you speak to? Did you talk to the family of the victim in Canada?"

"Yes," I said. "We're working with the family."

"What about his family. Where was he last seen?"

"Well. Here," I said. "Or this was the last place his name surfaced."

"Allegedly," he said. "Allegedly."

"Yes," I agreed. "Allegedly."

"Exactly. That's what I'm telling you."

"I understand that, sir. It would have been a violation of this man's rights had you detained him any longer, given there was no fingerprint match. But it's a strange anomaly. How did his information turn up thousands of miles away, thirty years later?"

"Someone saw a picture of the guy, somewhere on the FBI website or *Most Wanted*, and he favoured the guy. Someone saw a picture of someone that was wanted and thought this guy favoured him or looked similar to him."

"I was under the impression that ID or an information card was found."

"No . . . ," he said. "I can't recall anything like that happening."

"Okay," I said. "Well, thank you for returning the call. If anything else comes to mind, please text or phone us."

"Mm-hmm," he said.

We hung up.

The conversation ruffled me. Maybe it wasn't the guy. Maybe I was turning over rocks that had nothing under them. Yet this news had been out of the media for twenty-five years—how would Bax's name turn up here? *Unsolved Mysteries* had aired an episode on Ronald Bax in 1995, and there hadn't been a whisper since. Certainly not outside Canada, in rural Mississippi of all places. Somebody would have to trawl through every wanted notice in North America to find Bax's name: that explanation didn't add up to me either. We needed to talk to Sandy. And to Doug. However, it was starting to get late, and we had a meeting at the Stone Pony with the bartender from Rena Lara.

10.

WORM

The Stone Pony was a brick-walled pizza place with an alley-shaped bar at the back. Riley waved from the beer taps as we sat down. She wore metallic rose eyeshadow, which matched the sandy pink of her blouse, and her hair was meticulously woven into a fishtail braid.

As I review my notes from that evening, I remark how many times I described Riley as "careful." Her movements behind the bar struck me as swift and efficient—but careful. Her makeup jazzy—yet careful. Her attention oriented to us as she filled her drink orders—the way your attention orients to someone across the room, or a table, without needing to exchange eye contact. A peripheral awareness, which extended to other patrons too, leading her to swivel away from our chat when it was time to refill a beer and pivot back just as smoothly. She appeared mindful and observant.

Riley delivered the sleeve she'd been pouring, then rotated to greet us. "I'm very curious," she said.

Riley had lived in Rena Lara for only two years. By my calculation, the man with Bax's (alleged) information card would have been long gone by then. Still, she had lived in the wider area a long time, and maybe she knew someone who knew someone. Maybe she knew Doug and could advise us on how to approach him.

When I told Riley we were researching a Canadian man who might have passed through Rena Lara a few years ago, she didn't seem surprised.

"Do you mean Clinton?"

She registered my surprise.

"My husband's best friend used to work with him cutting trees. I'll text him now. He may not answer. I think he's flying back from Hawaii today."

"Did you ever meet Clinton?" I asked.

"I served him at the bar sometimes. He kept to himself." She hesitated, as if trying to word something tactfully. "I'm pretty friendly. I can get most regulars to open up to me. But he was private." She appeared pensive for a moment. "He always drank Miller Lite."

"When did he first show up in town?"

"At least five or six years ago," she said. "Maybe more. He was biking here from Alaska. I remember that. He'd gotten the ferry or something to Washington, and he was heading all the way to Florida."

Florida had been marked for us as a location of interest, given the comment of his cousin, who'd said, "If anything, he'd be in Florida," as well as the tip about the man at the Ontario campground "who had a place in Florida."

"So he was on a motorbike," I said, scribbling notes onto a napkin.

"No, no," Riley said. "He was riding a bicycle. From Alaska to Florida. And he stopped over in Rena Lara."

"He was riding a *bicycle*?"

"That's what I'm saying. There was something strange about him." She excused herself to fill a drink order.

I turned to Jasmine, both of us stunned. "It's brilliant," I said. "You don't need a driver's licence. You won't get pulled over for a speeding ticket. No one gives a shit about cyclists. He could travel completely under the radar."

And he was coming from Alaska, just across the border from

where Krystal was killed. When Riley returned, I clarified a few facts—aware my excitement was getting ahead of my judgment.

"I want to make sure we're talking about the same person," I said. "At one point he was detained by the Sheriff's Office."

"That's right."

"And he was staying with someone named Doug in Rena Lara?"

"I think so." It turned out that Doug's sister—the one without snakes in her head—was Riley's landlady.

"How would you describe his accent?" I asked.

"Northern," she said. "I'm pretty sure he was Canadian. But he was living in Alaska. And he was cycling to Florida when he stopped here. I guess he picked up some work."

"Did you ever see a tattoo?"

"I don't recall one, no."

"He had a tattoo of a winged horse. I think on his bicep."

It occurred to me that unless he wore tank tops, not many would have occasion to see his full bicep. ·

I pulled my phone out and searched for a photo of Ronald Bax—the clearest image of him online, with tousled blond hair, a thick moustache. I slid the phone across the bar to Riley.

She sucked in a breath. "That's him," she said. "Carbon copy. The same guy."

"Are you serious?" said Jasmine.

"I'm getting creeped out," Riley said. "Did you say he murdered someone?"

"Well *he* did," I said, pointing to the screen.

She raised the phone for a closer look. "Carbon copy," she said again. "The same face. Just older, you know. Less hair. But seriously—if you were to, what do you call it, superimpose this photograph . . . He looks the same."

Her certainty caught me off guard. I had been expecting a non-committal response to the photograph: a "maybe" or "could be."

"Hang on a second. I'll phone my husband. He knew Clinton better than I did. Maybe he can help." She ducked out from the bar.

"I don't believe it," I said.

"I do," said Jasmine.

When Riley returned a few minutes later, she said her husband remembered him. They'd partied together a few times. Once, they were drinking, and shirts came off. "You know how men are when booze gets involved. They were horsing around or whatever. Well, my husband saw his tattoo."

I slivered my eyes at her.

"The winged horse, right?" she went on. "My husband swears up and down he saw it."

She said her husband's cousin knew Clinton too. He worked at the beer and wine store around the corner. "He says y'all are welcome to drop by when you're done here."

"He's there now?" I said.

"Yup. Till eleven. His name's Worm." She laughed at our expressions. "His real name's Jonathan. We all call him Worm."

We found Worm behind a bulletproof screen. A sheet of corrugated metal formed a makeshift eave over the counter, so if you could ignore the fibre ceiling panels and carpet, the liquor store resembled a country shack.

Any hesitation or anxiety I had about meeting Worm dissolved as soon as we introduced ourselves. His age was hard to peg—in his twenties, I guessed. He was courteous and invited us to sit with him on his side of the window, yet his warmth never felt suggestive or charged.

We stayed with Worm for an hour. No patrons scanned the wine selection of the liquor store. The harder stuff was kept behind the counter, and customers lined up at the glass. Our conversation was studded by these interactions, paper bags sliding through the hole in the window. Worm leaned against a stool at the cash register. Jasmine perched on a stool by the door. I sat beside a muted television broadcasting a football game.

"So you used to work with Clinton?" I began.

"Actually, he worked for me," said Worm. "I hired him. I was running a country store out there in Rena Lara."

"Is that the country store that's still running?"

"It's still there, but closed now. The one running is a different one." Worm continued: "He came up riding a bike. He stopped at the store and it was almost dark. He was looking for the campground in Rosedale. That was a good twenty or twenty-five more miles. There was a guy out front who was one of my customers, and he invited him to go stay at his house."

That must have been Doug, I thought.

"Then he started living there," Worm went on. "He was in the store one day . . . it was the Fourth of July that year, and I was so swamped, I went out there and asked him, Hey man, do you want to work? He done told me he had worked in restaurants. I hired him on the spot. He helped me for three months. He winded up staying with that guy for at least two years. Then he stayed up here for a little bit at the Saunders Jewelry² store on the corner."

Saunders Jewelry was in Clarksdale, not Rena Lara. If Clinton wasn't running from anything in his life, I found his rootlessness strange. Didn't he have any attachments or responsibilities? It's one thing to travel when you reach a crossroads in your life. It's another to accidentally move in. Maybe when you're younger, and you're trying on different identities and homes—but in your fifties or sixties? I'm sure it happens, probably more often than I realize, but it stood out to me.

"I seen that page that was an FBI or most wanted page," Worm said. "One of my customers saw it, printed it out, and said doesn't that look like . . ." He trailed off. "Some girl found out about it and called in. That's when they picked him up and held him for two days. Checked everything and nothing came back on it. He ended up staying around here for another six months, seven months."

"Why did he leave?" Jasmine asked.

"There wasn't no work around here anymore and he didn't have anywhere to stay at the time. So I think he called his sister who was living in Arkansas at the time. She came and picked him up."

My ears perked up at the mention of a sister. Ronald Bax's sister in Michigan had regularly surfaced in the gossip mill of how Bax escaped, though she denied having any contact with him. Myles and I had made several attempts to get in touch with her but never heard back.

"We heard he was also cutting trees," I said.

"He did. He worked for Riley's husband's best friend, Clayton. I wonder how he got caught up—how he got set up with that." Worm funnelled his eyes at the carpet, as if ruminating on this question. "I know how it was," he said then. "One of Clayton's workers lived out there in Rena Lara. Where we all live."

I noticed he always said *out there* in Rena Lara, though he still lived there, and it was only fifteen miles away. The psychological distance appeared greater than the physical one.

"It's a tight-knit community," Worm explained. "If you need help, they'll find somebody to help you. Clint was out of work. He winded up going there and working with Clayton during the day. At the time when his sister came and got him, he was staying right here on the corner with the Saunders. There wasn't no work and nothing going on at the time and he ran out of money. So he called his sister and she came down here and picked him up. He didn't have his bike no more. Someone stole his bike. He couldn't take off on a bike. He was actually heading to the Keys. Key West. He almost had me talked into moving with him."

"What? Really?" I said, comprehending for the first time how close Worm and Clinton may have been. They seemed an unlikely match. Worm appeared to be in his twenties. Lanky build, sweep of hair under his ball cap. Maybe this is me as an older sister talking, but there was a sweetness to him. Even if Clinton had nothing to do with Ronald Bax, he was still a middle-aged partier, on the run from *something*, it would seem.

"Nearly went with him too," Worm said.

"Why?"

"I lost my job at the time and I was looking for something new. Something to do."

We nodded.

"I had a bit of money saved up. Clint said somebody had a job down there. I wanted to get out of Mississippi for a change."

"Right," I said, imagining Rena Lara could feel constraining for someone his age.

"Something told me not to do it."

"Oh?"

"I didn't want to go down there and the job not come through and be stuck in Florida with no family or nothing around. So I didn't go. And he didn't either. I guess he had nobody to take him. 'Cause like I said, his bike was stolen. And that's about it," said Worm. "He stayed around here for a good time. When I opened my own store, I hired him to do some painting. On the side, to help him out. Never had any problems with him. He was never confrontational. Real nice." He dipped into another thoughtful silence.

"When I saw that . . . ," he started. "It looked like him and everything. But they also said he had a tattoo. I never saw the tattoo. A friend of mine he was living with swore he had the same tattoo. I never saw it, so I'm not sure on that one."

"Do you mean Doug?"

"Yep, Doug."

"So Doug is the one he was living with."

"Doug is the one who told him he could stay that first night and he ended up staying with him for two years."

"Are you still friends with Doug?" Jasmine asked.

"Yep," Worm said with a bit of a shrug.

"Do you think he'd be willing to talk to us?"

"I don't see why not," said Worm. "I just don't have his number on hand right now. I can find it tonight or tomorrow. If y'all want it."

"We would love that," I said. "We know around where he lives, but I don't know how he'd take to us knocking on his door."

"No, that's not Doug. He's . . . He don't meet a stranger. That's just how Doug is. You know what I mean? That's why he invited Clint to stay with him."

"How old would you say this guy was?" I asked. "Clint."

"It's hard to tell because he was already whited. Grey hair. Late fifties, early sixties, I guess."

Ronald Bax was born in 1961, making him fifty-eight at the time of our conversation with Worm.

"He was probably five eight, five seven, somewhere around there. Skinny. I want to say blue eyes but I could be wrong. Real sandy white hair. I don't believe I don't have a picture of him some-where . . ."

The height and eye colour both matched RCMP records for Ronald Bax.

"*Do* you have a photo?" I asked, not masking my eagerness.

"I know I ain't got one but I bet there are some pictures around, because he was around too many people and too many parties not to be in a picture."

"Would Doug have a photo?" Jasmine asked.

"If he don't he might know someone who might."

Worm had been looking at his phone, as if to find a picture, or the number of someone who might have one. Then he put the phone down. "The girl who Doug was married to at that time, she didn't trust him," he said. "After Doug— After they went to work or something, his bag was there. So she went through the bag and seen an ID and everything. She didn't want to be there by herself with Doug gone and him there. So she looked through to see if she found anything alarming but it wasn't so."

I found this an odd contradiction—what ID did she find if it "wasn't so"? And if it "wasn't so," why would Sandy have called the police? I liked Worm from our conversation so far, but I didn't take everything he said at face value. I got the sense he wanted to protect his friend.

"We heard she found ID that belonged to the guy wanted in Canada," I said.

"I don't know about that," said Worm. "Not her. The ID she found had Clinton on it. Clinton, I want to say Hill. He swore up and down that his family was . . . He was a military brat. That's the reason he moved so much. He went there, lived there. Every time we talked it was a different story where he lived."

"Do you remember those stories?" I asked.

"I want to say he lived in West Virginia on the base, right before him and his dad got into it or something. He lived in Florida one time years ago, working for a fishing boat. Like a dockhand. That's when he moved to Alaska. He stayed in Alaska for two years and swore up and down he still had a place in Alaska. When he left Alaska he came on a boat to Washington and left from there. He rode a bike all the way down and came up toward us and was headed to the Keys."

I waited for him to continue.

"That's all I knew of him," Worm said. "He never did mention any family. But then I found out he had a sister that he'd been talking to on the phone, and the only reason I know that is because he was living with Doug, and she was sending him money for his phone bill when he wasn't working and stuff like that."

I wondered who this woman was—a sister, like Worm said? Or a friend? Confidante? Lover?

"I think she was in Little Rock," Worm said. "It's definitely in Arkansas, I know that for a fact," he said. "He had no way of getting to her. He couldn't meet her."

Sure enough, Little Rock is 240 kilometres from Rena Lara. But the Arkansas border is only on the other side of Desoto Lake, which is right next to Rena Lara. You could cross state lines from Rena Lara in under ten minutes.

"Did Clint drive?" I asked.

"No, he came up on a bike."

"But he was able to drive?"

"Yeah, he was able to drive."

"But he didn't have a licence?"

"He had a li— He had ID that had Clinton Hill on it, but I don't know if it was an ID card or a driver's licence."

I noticed how careful he was to stick to this point.

"What he was doing was working his way to the Keys, staying at each campground," Worm said, but then a customer came in. He served the customer and turned back to us. "After that, nothing else. When he got arrested and all that, nothing else was said about it."

"Did you ever notice burns on his hands?" Jasmine asked. "Or anything about his hands?"

"Not that I remember," Worm said. "He helped me cook and everything. I was hesitant about that at first. What made me hire him that time—usually I wouldn't do that. But I was so swamped running the store on my own for six months. It just got open. I was putting in over a hundred hours a week, seven days a week, sun-up to sundown," he said. "He showed me how to make homemade pizza, bread. I never saw any burns on his hands or anything. But there are lots of things that aren't there anymore 'cause I had a wreck three years ago. Bad wreck. I was in a wheelchair for three months."

"I'm so sorry to hear that," I said.

"2015. Head-on collision with an eighteen-wheeler going about sixty."

I winced.

"You remember an incredible amount," Jasmine said. "I would never be able to tell you had a wreck."

"It's not really the older things," he said. "It's the recent things. I never noticed it until months later." He left us to serve a customer. When he finished, I asked what Clinton's accent was like.

"Northern," said Worm.

I nodded, wondering how northern his accent would sound if he grew up in Virginia in the 1960s. I suppose it would depend on what part of Virginia, and where his parents were from.

"But it wasn't that bad," Worm said. "Not like you could tell."

"What's my accent like?" I asked with a smile.

"Yours isn't bad either," Worm said, reddening faintly.

"I've been teaching her *fixin' to*," Jasmine said.

"Prob'ly so," I said, with a gentle twang, and we all laughed.

"Did he tell you anything else about his background?" I asked. "Why he turned up?"

"He never went into what he did," Worm said. "He never really got paid by a cheque, I guess. It seemed like he worked for cash. Every job he got was under the table. He never said anything about no big company. The only thing I remember is the boating thing in Florida. Early nineties, I want to say it was, when that was going on. That's the reason he was thinking about going back to work on the docks. But I don't think he ever went. I bet you he's still in Arkansas with his sister."

"What was he doing on the dock?" Jasmine asked.

"He was working on the boats. He would take people fishing. Charter boats, bait and hook, cleaning fish, that sort of thing. Off the Keys. That's what he said. I don't remember anything else."

"If you had to guess, he'd be in Arkansas?"

"I'd bet a hundred— I'm a hundred percent sure that he's still in Arkansas."

"What makes you so sure?"

"It's the only family he had."

"What if Clint made some money and kept on toward the Florida Keys?" I asked.

"What I noticed about Clint—if you keep him occupied, he ain't going anywhere. As long as he can work and make a dollar there, he's happy. He was only going to stay a couple days, then a couple days went to two years, which was crazy."

I agreed that even if Clinton Hill had nothing to do with Ronald Bax, it seemed odd he had nowhere to go or be.

"I can see him still being there unless he and his sister got into it," Worm said. "Like I said, she was calling him every week. Checking on him."

"Do you remember her name?"

"No. Only reason I know that is Sandy remembers his sister calling all the time, sending him money. I don't know if it was Western Union, or— And you know what was weird. He had an Alaska cell phone number. I wish I still had my cell phone, my old one. I had his number programmed."

"Is there any way to find that number? It might be in your contacts."

"No. I had a flip phone back then."

"Well, you said he came from Alaska. Makes sense that he had an Alaska phone number," I said.

"That's what made me think everything that came out of his

mouth might be real. 'Cause he said he was from Alaska and had an Alaska number. But after a while, you start to wonder. 'Cause like I said, he never did leave. Like he was satisfied just making ten bucks a day. No ambitions to do something else. He would settle for anything."

"Do you know if his sister had any kids?" Jasmine asked. "Was she married?"

"I don't know. Doug might know."

"We don't have Doug's number," I reminded him.

"I can get it. Just give me one sec . . ." He began scrolling through his phone again.

"Thank you for talking to us," I said. "It's been a strange day."

"Mine was strange too," he said as he tapped a number onto his screen and held the phone to his ear. "When my cousin called and told me y'all were over there . . . Hey Christine," he said. "It's Worm." Christine was Doug's niece. "You got Doug's number by chance? Oh good. Remember that thing your brother printed off about old Clint? I got two ladies doing a documentary about it down here."

I raised my eyebrows. At no point had we told anyone we were shooting a documentary.

"They're trying to get in touch with Doug," Worm went on. "I thought that was it," he said after Christine recited the number. "Just wanted to double-check. It's been a while. Hey, Christine— you don't know anyone who might have a picture of Clint, like from a party or a gathering we might have had? Oh, I know. I just remember all them get-togethers we might have had at Doug's house. I knew there must have been some pictures taken some-where." He hung up. "His phone's messed up right now," he told us. "I can text him but not call. Let me just text him. Christine's going to look through some of her pictures and see if he's in a shot. If she finds something, she'll send it to me."

"Did Clint have any hobbies?" I asked as Worm texted Doug. "Things he did on the side?"

"Not really," Worm said. "He was more into cooking than anything. But he didn't mind being outdoors."

"You mentioned someone found a wanted listing," I said. "Who was that?"

"The girl I just talked to, her brother. I don't know what made him do that."

"There are a lot of wanted people in North America," I said. "It's strange he would . . ."

Worm continued my thought. "It's strange you would just pick someone. I guess 'cause he was staying with Doug, his uncle. He was around us at the time."

This detail was confusing to me—I thought it was Sandy who found the wanted listing. Either way, the logic didn't seem to hold. How do you stumble across a wanted listing when the case had been out of the media for decades?

"I can get his number too," Worm said. "Chase Mayor. He's the one that looked him up and everything and found it." Worm glanced at his phone. "Doug texted me back. He ain't paid his bill yet, that's all."

He called Christine again to ask for her brother's number. When he reminded her that it was Chase who found the wanted ad, I heard her say through the receiver, "No, it wasn't."

"Yeah, it was. That was Chase who found it," Worm said.

"No, it wasn't," Christine repeated.

"Oh well," said Worm.

At this point, her voice grew too faint to discern words.

"They're just doing a documentary," Worm said. After a moment he looked up at me and Jasmine. "Did y'all pull up in front of Doug's house today and take a photo?"

I laughed uneasily. We did. Or I did. After Walt Madison

showed us the house in Rena Lara, Jasmine parked a few metres away and I walked back to snap a photo. A woman had stepped onto her porch, right next door to Doug's, and asked what I thought I was doing.

"We weren't sure that was his house," I answered.

"With the bicycles?" Worm said.

I paused, hesitant to out myself for taking photos without asking.

"Tricycles."

"Yeah, it was them," Worm said into the phone. "They didn't know it was his house."

I exchanged an uncomfortable glance with Jasmine.

Worm said goodnight to Christine, then jotted something on a scrap of paper. "This is Doug's number," he said. "You can text him, but you can't call him."

"Thank you," I said.

"What are y'all doing when I get off?" he said.

"You tell me," said Jasmine.

Again, the three of us laughed.

"I'm going that way when I go home at ten," he said. "If you want to come with me, I can introduce you."

It felt late to be knocking on someone's door, but I urgently wanted to talk to this person. What if this was our only chance? "We'd love to come with you. Thank you."

The conversation drifted back to Clinton.

"He's a man who stayed under the radar," Worm said.

"Sounds like he didn't have a social security number or anything like that," I said.

"I don't think so either," said Worm.

"I understand too . . . ," I said, my turn now to trail off. He was going out of his way to help us, and I wanted to acknowledge that this whole thing must be pretty weird for him.

"I'm sure he was a nice guy. It must be strange having these people come from out of town asking about him."

"Not really," said Worm. "Toward the end it was nerve-racking."

"Nerve-racking?" I repeated, struck by his choice of words, given the context of why we were here asking questions.

"I couldn't get away from him," Worm explained. "When we got off work, usually I'd come to town, go to Kroeger's, Walmart, get everything I needed for the next day. Tomatoes, bread. He would always want a ride. At first I was like, okay, that's fine. But when he wanted a ride, I couldn't go to a friend's house, 'cause I couldn't take him with me. He didn't know none of them. It kind of got nerve-racking. I couldn't go anywhere without him wanting to go. Finally I just— He'd say, you going to town. I'd say, no, I'm going straight home, where you going, I'll drop you off."

He glanced at his phone again—Doug had replied. "He said yeah. He'll be up. He'll be at his mama's house—that house with the tricycles. Now this is a weird family, I'll tell you that up front."

"You want to come in with us?" Jasmine asked.

"Oh, it ain't nothing like that. He ain't gonna hurt you. It's just . . . his mom is crazy. Not like bad crazy. Just religious crazy. I've seen her. When my mom got sick. I looked out my front yard and she's out there on her hands and knees sitting there praying in my front yard. Just weird. I don't know. You'll see. Doug's the same way. Not religious. But he's butt wild. Likes to party. Likes to hang out, carry on. The whole family's weird."

"Did we upset his sister by being outside their house?" I asked.

"She didn't say. You weren't at hers, you was at Doug's mama's house, the one next door." He began mapping the lots in the air with his finger. "This house you was at—Doug lived in a trailer that was right here. They sold that to somebody. That's where Clint would have been."

"So the land's still there but the trailer's not?"

"Trailer's still there," he said. "They sold that too. All that was family-owned. About half them folks live out there, most of them are kin. I learned that the hard way. You don't ever open your mouth. I would put my foot in mine all the time. So many people are kin out there."

I thought about how Worm swayed between admitting something didn't add up and affirming Clint was a nice guy, with the correct ID.

"Should we call you Jonathan or Worm?" I asked him.

He blushed, swatting the back of his neck with his hand. "It's a childhood nickname I'm stuck with. It don't bother me. I've had teachers call me that."

"We'll call you whatever you want us to call you," I said.

"Jonathan's fine."

11.

DOUG

A wiry man in a white T-shirt greeted all three of us from the front porch. Jonathan had decided to drop in as well.

"Y'all get in here!" Doug said, a glint of laughter in his eyes.

"We come bearing wine," I told him, passing the bottle in a paper bag. He had hinted to Jonathan that he had a hankering for merlot.

"Oh aren't you a sweetheart," he said, grasping my hands with both of his.

He led us inside, where a woman smiled at us from the kitchen counter. Jasmine and I had seen her the day before, withdrawing money from an ATM at the Country Store.

"This is Brooke," Doug said. Brooke was Sandy's cousin, we would learn.

"What do y'all want with Clinton?" Doug asked.

"Yeah, what would you want with *him*?" Brooke echoed.

"You mean Clint out back?" said Doug.

"Out back?" I asked. "You mean he's here?" The blood palpably drained from my face.

"We can go get him, if you like," Brooke said.

Jasmine and I locked eyes.

"That's a different Clinton," said Doug. "What Clinton are y'all looking for?"

How many Clintons could there be? Unless "Clint out back"

was like "Larry up the hill"—a fond, locational abbreviation. "A guy who passed through Rena Lara several years ago," I said. "On a bicycle."

Doug guided us into the living room. Someone had affixed a plank of wood to the ceiling, which read in hand-printed Sharpie: *Don't ever make your Mama cry.* The Paddle, Doug called it, which his mother had used to beat him and his sisters when they misbehaved.

Jasmine and I perched on the brown sofa, next to a considerable buck torso that veered from the wall. The torso, head, and rack filled three-quarters of the wall, from carpet to low stucco ceiling.

Doug sunk into an armchair and hooked his chin on his hand. "Clinton, Clinton . . . ," he said. "Oh, you mean Clint! Old Clint! I haven't thought of him in ages. Aw, Clint," he repeated.

His confusion puzzled me, because Jonathan had told him why we were coming, and Doug had asked what we wanted with Clint. But maybe there *were* two Clintons. The prospect that the man I had been searching for, Ronald Bax or not, might be "out back" within "getting" distance was so inconceivable that I took Doug's word for it. Of course there were two Clintons—it wasn't so unusual a name. Was it?

Throughout our conversation, Brooke remained in the kitchen, watching from a stool at the counter where the merlot also sat, unopened.

Doug was telling us about Clinton's sister from Arkansas. "There was another sister, too," he said, "from . . . is there a Juniper, Alaska?"

"There's a Juneau," I said.

"Juneau, yeah," he said. "She came here and brought him credit cards and stuff. That's how he did it for a while. Oh, Clint," he said again, a note of affection in his voice. "One crazy guy."

She brought him credit cards? That was more than wiring money now and then, though I wasn't sure how reliable Doug's memory was when it came to details.

Doug told a similar story to Jonathan's, with a few added details: how he had been sitting in front of the Country Store, drinking a beer. Clinton pulled up on his bicycle and asked if they thought the church would let him stay on their property in a tent. "Yeah, the church will let you, but the mosquitoes ain't gonna let you," Doug had replied. "They were bad, man."

"And them gnats," Jonathan agreed. "Them bull gnats were bad that year."

"What year was that?" I asked.

"Year of the flood," he said. "2011. A hundred-year flood, we had. Anyhow, I told him I live down here, I told him the address of the mailbox here. And sure enough, he come down here and showed up. We hung out with him. Man, he was so proper and everything."

"Proper?"

"Yeah, man. He was a cyclist. He spoke well. But you could hear him scream from here to them woods. He wasn't here five minutes, my cousin tells him, jump in the back of the truck, I'll take you to the woods and show you some stuff. I could hear Clinton screaming from here."

"Wait. Why was he screaming?"

Jonathan filled me in, which he'd continue to do throughout the evening, every time Doug detoured into an anecdote and didn't hear me ask for clarification. "'Cause Colin scared the crap out of him," he said. "He shot across the highway in a truck and went straight across the field with Clint in the back."

"He had a good time," Doug said. "He ended up staying here over two years. Two or three years."

"And then he helped me in 2015," Jonathan said. "When he

helped paint my store. That was the last time I actually seen him."

"He worked for Mike Wilson too," Doug said.

"Cutting trees?"

"No. A different one. He was working for a farmer out here. The one that owns the bigger store. Was it y'all out here taking pictures?"

The abrupt change of subject startled me. I laughed awkwardly. "It was me," I said. "I'm sorry if that upset your sister. We're working on this project. I wasn't sure which one your house was." When no one responded, I repeated: "I apologize if it was alarming."

"Well, we don't have police out here," Doug said. He laughed. "They don't never show up."

I nodded, taking this in.

"Where y'all from?" he asked.

"I'm from Canada," I said.

"I'm from Texas," Jasmine said.

He told us he was originally from Detroit, but his family moved here when he was three. He returned to Detroit when he was older, to see "what other folks were out there," but came back to Mississippi ten or twelve years later. "I been here, this same house, everything, all my life," he said. "My sister's next door. My other sister's across the field. These are all my cousins," he said, gesturing out the window. "Old Clint. God."

"Do you remember his sister's name?" I asked.

"No."

"All those get-togethers he was at," Jonathan said. "I know somebody had to take some pictures."

"Sandy took all them shit when she left," Doug said.

"Women tend to take more photos than men," Jasmine said.

Doug laughed. "We had the mug shot of him. Sandy had him locked up."

"Was that an old mug shot or a new one?"

When I said "old mug shot," I'd meant of Ronald Bax—the first of several occasions I would realize a fundamental gap in our communication. For Doug and Jonathan, Clint was Clint, the friendly if eccentric cyclist from Canada or Alaska. For me, he could also be Ronald Bax.

"The new one, from right here. They took him to jail and they had his mug shot on file. They saw him as a killer somewhere like in Canada, and they came picked him up."

"Christine was telling me it wasn't Chase," Jonathan said. "But wasn't it Chase that brought our attention to the paperwork?"

"Sandy," said Doug definitively. "It was Sandy. Boy, that was the dirtiest thing I ever seen."

"Did Sandy go through his belongings?" I asked.

"I'm pretty sure," Doug said.

"Sandy made me come over there with her," Jonathan said. "She felt uncomfortable at first."

"Well, man, wouldn't you?" said Doug with a laugh. "But that was— It was nothing big." The muscles of his jaw clenched. "Her being deceitful, hateful," he added.

"That whole time I knew Clint, I never took him to be that type of a person," Jonathan said. "But people change over the years. You never know."

"I heard he went to Miami," Doug said.

"Well, one time he wanted me to go with him to the Keys, remember?" Jonathan said. "I was going to sell my truck."

"What makes you think he went to Miami?" I asked.

"He was, uh— He was kind of a partier," said Doug.

"He wanted to go from Alaska all the way to the Keys on his bike," Jonathan said. "But we kind of slowed his motion up."

"I left the bike outside in the rain, where it would rust up, so he couldn't leave," admitted Doug with a loose smile. "I liked him, man. He was pretty cool."

"Did he have any hobbies or interests?" I asked.

"That son of a bitch could cook," Doug said. "He made the best bread you ever seen in your life."

"Oh yeah?"

"I had the convection oven, brand new," Doug said. "My dad bought it for me. Clint was the one who tested it out because I never knew nothing about fancy cooking. Oh, he could cook up some stuff. Nothing I ever heard of. But he would lay it out on the table and I'd eat it. It was good, whatever it was." He paused, remembering. "I'll never forget about that bread. Everybody met him here."

"Everybody pretty much liked him, let's be honest," said Jonathan.

They discussed how old he might be now, how he might have been old enough then to be on social security—sixty-two or sixty-five—because he always had his own money.

"How did he get his money?" I asked.

Jonathan and Doug answered at the same time: "His sister."

"The one that's in Arkansas is the one that kept his money," Doug said.

"What did she look like?"

"Big woman," Doug said. "Way bigger than him. Tall, and kind of broad. Red hair. He was grey when he got here, so I don't know what his real colour was."

"The other sister from Juneau—he was as big as her. They looked like they had a rough life."

I nodded. Neither description matched Bax's sister, who is blond and looks like she spends her winters skiing with family.

"They didn't stay long," Doug said. "They just brought stuff to him."

"Did you think it was strange?" I asked. "If he had a place in Alaska, why did he leave it?"

"Well, like I said, he wanted to ride his bike all the way to Key West."

Yet he waylaid himself in Rena Lara for several years? It didn't feel like the moment to emphasize this point. It was clear Doug didn't believe Clinton was Ronald Bax. To linger too long on the counter-narrative would suggest I believed his ex-wife: delicate territory.

"He told me what he did before," Doug continued, "but damn, I can't remember what the hell it was."

Jonathan said, "I know one time he said he worked in Miami, or around that area, off fish boats."

"He could have done that in Alaska," said Doug. "How the heck did y'all hear about Clinton?" he asked.

"He was known as a sculptor," I said, referring to Ronald Bax. This was somewhat true—Bax was a sculptor—but it didn't answer Doug's question. His words that the police "don't never show up" were ringing in my mind. I wasn't sure how much to tell him.

"He's an artist," said Jonathan. "Not Clinton but that guy they're thinking—that guy we thought— You know what I mean."

"There's only one Clint," Doug said.

"The other guy," said Jonathan.

"He's a sculptor?" Doug said.

"Well, he *was*," I said.

"The one who was accused of the murder," Jonathan went on. "The one that's wanted. Not—"

"Oh, the one they *thought* was Clint," said Doug.

"Yeah," Jonathan said. "That's what they're trying to connect. That's how . . ."

"Oh, you're all trying to find that old boy?" Doug asked.

"Well," I started, "It's just . . ."

"He's wanted for a crime," Doug said. I wasn't sure if the message was "good luck" or "be careful."

"You have to understand," I said. "It's been thirty years. The only time his name surfaced has been in this area." I felt myself over-explaining, worried Doug's hospitality would turn. With Doug's chair perpendicular to our sofa, it was easy to talk without looking at each other. Doug's gaze generally fell in the centre of the room, but now and then, I felt his lucid attention on us. "So did Clinton hunt?" I asked, changing the subject.

"No, he couldn't hunt," Doug said. "He wasn't big enough to pull the mud. He went with us."

"Deer hunting," Jonathan clarified. "Illegally. Out on the truck."

So he did hunt?

"I always thought he was a damn cook," Doug said. "He had to cook somewhere to learn all that."

"Oh yeah, he worked at a restaurant," Jonathan said. "He learned most of the bread making and noodles and all that—he learned from an Italian woman."

"I bet you Winston would know too," Doug said. "He lived with Winston and took care of him. Winston had a wreck down here. I told Clint to move out of that truck and move in with Winston and take care of him, 'cause he broke his neck."

"Not the same wreck you had . . . ," Jasmine said to Jonathan.

"No, I had a wreck two years after that."

"We have troubles staying on the highway," said Doug.

"We do a lot of stupid stuff," said Jonathan.

"We're tough as wet leather," said Doug.

"So he learned to cook from an Italian woman," I said.

"That's what he told me," said Jonathan. "The bread and fresh pasta noodles. Homemade pizza."

"I took one of his pizzas and put it on the grill there," said Doug. "Man, that guy could cook. I loved that little fellow."

Jonathan said, "The whole time I knew him, I never knew Clint to get angry or mad."

"He was around here five years, I bet," said Doug. "He lived in my trailer two years after living with me. Then I moved over to Veronica's. Two or three years, and he was still here. Must have been here at least five years. They picked him up from Winston's, I think," he continued. "They kept him in there three days. They said that was to process him and make sure. That poor little fellow got tortured in there. They felt so bad they took him to McDonald's after. He was good at painting and stuff like that."

Jasmine nudged me. She pointed up. Six ladybugs roamed the ceiling above the sofa where she and I were sitting.

"Ladybugs," I said somewhat stupidly.

"We have cotton fields in front of the house," Doug said. "When they pick the cotton, they come inside to find a place to live."

"They're actually Asian beetles," said Jonathan. "They'll bite you."

"I never see ladybugs," said Jasmine, gazing with me at the ceiling. She knew about my coincidences with red animals.

"Whatever happened to the guy who . . . ," began Doug.

I found it fascinating that both he and Jonathan preferred abstractions whenever Ronald Bax came up. *The guy who . . .* Neither seemed able to say "murdered."

"They don't know," said Jonathan.

"They haven't caught him," I said. "It's been nearly thirty years."

"Did it happen in the vicinity of where y'all are at?"

"Nowhere near me, actually," I said. "He was on the other side of the country. Very close to Alaska."

"That guy had tattoos all over him," said Doug. "Clint never had tattoos at all on him. And we been drunk a bunch. We partied, clothes, no clothes. Everybody saw everybody. Didn't mean to be. But tattoos on the little fella. I didn't see none."

On Ronald Bax's wanted listing, the RCMP mentions only one tattoo—the winged horse on his upper arm. Jonathan had suggested Doug had seen the tattoo, but maybe he was thinking of his cousin, Riley's husband.

"We walked around without shirts on," Jonathan agreed.

"Working and painting."

The conversation veered toward where Clinton had come from, and how he'd gotten around.

"We got to figuring one time he was telling us a fib about going on that bicycle," said Doug. "We come find out his sister brought him a good distance. I guess he got tired. Dropped him up on the bridge."

"I remember that," Jonathan said, "'cause for a long time he made out like he rode it from Washington State."

"He was in Portland," said Doug.

"What was he doing in Portland?" I asked.

"I want to say some kind of fishing," said Jonathan.

"One time he said he worked on one of them boats," said Doug. "What is it, lobster or . . . up there in Alaska."

"King crab?" Jasmine offered. "Alaska king crab?"

"Alaska king crab," agreed Doug. "He was on one of them Alaska king crab boats."

This detail—particular to Alaska—made me wonder again if Jonathan had confused the Florida detail. Maybe his work off the docks had been in Alaska in the nineties, not Miami, as Doug also suggested.

"Oh, I hadn't thought about him in so long," said Doug. "I thought y'all . . . I thought y'all were talking about old crazy Clinton over here all this time."

Brooke, silent until now, chimed in from the kitchen. "Yeah, I was thinking what's so interesting about him."

"I remember him saying something about working in a restaurant there in Alaska in the busy season," said Jonathan. "I remember him saying their busy time of year was because of the cruise liners. That's how the town would make their money."

I knew what he was talking about. I grew up in Victoria, one of the southern destinations on the Alaska cruise route. You knew what areas of downtown to avoid when they pulled in.

"That damn boy," said Doug, laughing at a fresh memory. "He'd come down my hallway, drunker than hell, out of the shower. There was like ten folks sittin' in here, and you could see straight into that trailer. He'd move like a bullet."

"I can tell you were good friends with him," I said.

"We had fun," said Doug. "I taught him stuff he ain't never seen, like hunting, how we do it. We're not allowed on private property so we wait till night and go. Lord, we had fun. I took him to Clarksdale and showed him everything. He stayed up there for a while, with Manny or Moe Saunders."

"Was that at the end of his time here?" I asked.

"Yeah, toward the end. He left without me knowing," said Doug.

"Really?" I said. "He didn't say goodbye?"

"I was in Louisiana, I think. At my daughter's. They had a flood in Louisiana that had done in her house. That was three years ago, four years ago."

"More than that because you went before my wreck. It's been four years since I had that."

"I was out of pocket, and I came back," said Doug.

"I didn't even know he was gone either," said Jonathan. "I remember somebody told me his sister picked him up."

I found this odd. If Clinton was just a middle-aged wanderer on a bike quest from Alaska to the Florida Keys, why did he leave so discreetly?

"I didn't keep up with him all the time," said Doug. "My kids had their house flooded."

"I think he got tired of being around Manny and them, 'cause they're all crazy," said Jonathan.

Doug shook his head. "All this time, I was thinking about this other Clinton back here."

And again, Brooke chimed in from the kitchen stool. "I couldn't figure it out," she said.

"Hell, leave a number or something," said Doug. "I'll call and tell you. His stuff is either here or out there in my shed."

He'd left his things here?

"What kind of stuff do you have?" asked Jasmine.

"Whatever he left here in my trailer. I had to clean my trailer out to sell it to that guy who bought it next door."

"Do you mind if we take a look?" I asked.

"Look in my shed?" Doug chuckled, as if that might be easier said. But he agreed—he led us outside. It was getting toward midnight. It was total country darkness outside—no streetlights. Only the light from Doug's flashlight and our cell phones.

The shed was chained and padlocked. He unwound the chain and heaved open the door, poking through invisible items in the black. "All that crap there," he said, "that's my ex-wife's and his stuff." His flashlight fell on a heap of clothes, tools, equipment, junk that occupied most of the shed's volume, from floor to roof. "Under all that," he said.

Everyone laughed.

"I gotta clean this out," he said. "Leave an address and I'll mail it to you. I don't need it."

"Is it clothing?" I asked.

"Little bit of everything. Letters he had wrote, the addresses y'all probably want. The sisters. All that."

Letters? Part of me wanted to go through everything right then—just in case we couldn't get hold of Doug the next day. The prospect that we might be this close to Clinton's stuff and unable to search it was tormenting. But it was late, and we'd have to work with only our cell phones and Doug's flashlight.

"Sounds like a daytime project," said Jasmine. "We can help you clean it out."

"We can give it a whirl, if you want," he said. "I'm ninety-nine percent sure it's right in there." He gestured back to the undistinguishable heap.

"We'll come back to you tomorrow," I said. "What time are you up?"

"Whenever you want."

12.

LADYBUGS

As Jasmine and I approached the cotton fields the next morning, something began thwacking our windshield. It was a superb day: cloudless, the sky a rinsing blue, over twenty degrees—but inside the Jeep, it sounded like hail was pelting down. We found Doug already outside, unlooping the chain from the shed. I jumped out, and something flicked past my ear. Then my collarbone. Then my forearm. We were surrounded by ladybugs. When I say "surrounded," I mean: thousands and thousands of them, the air abuzz with the hum of their wings, the patter of their bodies pummelling the tin roof of the shed. It sounded like rain. They disappeared into our hair, our armpits. I put my long-sleeve shirt back on. Later, when I went to the bathroom, I found them seeded in the crotch of my underwear.

"Ladybugs are out," said Doug, greeting us both with a hug.

"No kidding," I said.

"I've never seen this many before," said Jasmine.

"They're bad today," he agreed.

In this way, we began our work: ferrying boxes from Doug's shed to the rusted truck trailer that sat in his driveway, all the while occupied in a business of swatting, wriggling, head-banging in an attempt to loosen the bugs from our scalps. Doug paused now and then to brush them off my back. "They're all over you," he'd say.

He did most of the heavy lifting. I combed through the boxes of files and envelopes on the trailer. Jasmine filmed the unpacking:

the plastic boxes of old leather boots, glassless picture frames, slippers, hairbrushes, handbags, files, letters (none of them from Clint), all teeming with beetles. Racks of old clothes. A VHS tape of the 1996 film *Alaska* ("A missing father. A desperate search. An unforgettable adventure," the cover reads).

Doug shared bits and pieces—how his mother never recovered from her fall. She had passed away the month before, but she hadn't been well for a while. He had enjoyed the wine we brought him—he took it to work, painting the Pentecostal church next door. He didn't sleep much, he admitted. We found family letters. His divorce papers. Company invoices. Old prescriptions. None of them Clinton's. At one point Doug mentioned he burned a bunch of stuff when Clint left.

We did find Clinton's old tackle box (empty) and garbage sacks of his clothes. He wore plaid pyjamas, pullovers, narrow-waisted khakis. We found a bike helmet: a rounded skater style, heavy and silver, scuffed at the back. We found an LG phone with the memory card removed. After a few hours, wrestling with Doug's junk, and the beetles, we volunteered to drive to the Country Store for refreshments.

The ladybugs had seeped into the Jeep; they filled the cracks between the window glass and the frame like a sort of animate *kintsugi,* the Japanese art of repairing broken pottery with gold. But when we stepped out of the car at the store, no more than four hundred metres down the road, the air was still. Not one ladybug. The beetles had swarmed within a hundred metres on either side of Doug's house.

We purchased a six-pack of Miller Lite for Doug and Coke for ourselves. I wondered for the first time how old he thought we were. With our backpacks on, no makeup, drinking cans of Coke, we looked barely eighteen.

We combed through items for another hour or so, but it was

obvious by this point that we wouldn't find a trove of letters from Clinton to his sister, or any other relevant documents. We'd been searching for hours, and only the clothes, helmet, and phone seemed to have any relevance to Clinton. All the paperwork belonged to Doug. And anyway, he'd mentioned burning some of Clinton's things. Which itself was an odd detail to share: if you were to keep garbage sacks of his clothing for years, you're presumably not burning things out of spite or to clear space. Was there something that Clinton hadn't wanted other people to see? Or was this detail like some of the others—half-remembered, blurred with other memories?

The phone was of interest to me, but useless without the memory card. I felt grateful for Doug's help, but increasingly ill at ease. I hadn't felt so at first—maybe thanks to the adrenaline, or my hope of finding something that might tell us more about Clinton's identity. But now I felt the growing sense that we wouldn't find anything, that Doug was quite literally "performing" the search for our sake. When we eventually left, Doug said he would keep going—he'd been meaning to clean the shed for ages. If he found anything, he assured us, he would call us. I had no reason not to believe him. But when we returned shortly after—we'd realized it would be prudent to take something with us on the fractional chance it contained a hair root or sweat with Clinton's DNA— Doug had stuffed everything back in the shed. Of course he had gone through his shed for our benefit. But to watch him spend hours disembowelling it, for him to say that he would keep going, that he would call us if he found anything, and then to find the shed chained and locked forty minutes later—it felt disjointed.

This time, Jasmine stayed in the Jeep. I walked warily down the driveway with another bottle of wine—a thank-you gift.

Doug looked oddly touched, if not sheepish. "Aw, y'all didn't have to," he said, climbing down the steps to meet me. Brooke was over again, I noticed, drinking a beer on the deck. She nodded at me.

"You spent hours taking apart your shed for us," I told him. "We really appreciate it."

"Oh, I needed to do it anyway," he said.

"You said before that I could keep the bike helmet . . ."

"Oh," he said, glancing toward the shed.

"Is it back in there?"

"I can open it again."

"You're sure?"

"Sure," he said, walking over to the shed, slipping the key in the padlock, uncoiling the chain. He opened the doors to reveal a wall of junk, as if he had simply crammed everything back inside. The bike helmet was perched on a stack of garbage bags in the corner. I picked it up. In the end, Doug offered me two of Clint's pullovers, and the phone too.

I was disappointed not to have found a letter between Clinton and his sister, if only to know her name, to be able to contact her, but I was also feeling ready to leave Rena Lara. Doug's home had felt outside time somehow—like you could drop by, as Clinton had, and two years would pass. I was anxious to move on with the interviews. We had plans to meet with Sandy the next day, and I was eager to hear what she had to say. But first I would stop by Saunders Jewelry in Clarksdale, where Clinton had stayed during his last months in the area.

"Thank you, girls," Doug said when we shared our final goodbye.

"Thank *you*," I said. "We really appreciate your help."

"Y'all let me know when you come back to town," he said. "You know where I live."

Brooke had been quietly watching. "You girls be careful," she said.

Those words had become a refrain. Almost everyone we spoke to bid farewell by saying "careful."

Saunders Jewelry was a two-storey corner building, beating turquoise, the words *Saunders* and *Jewelry* on two peeling signs. Inside
looked not unlike Doug's shed: myriad wires, boxes, cabinets,
lamps. A man was at work behind the glass counter. Sandy grey
hair in a mullet, beard whitened at the chin, a weathered, pallid
complexion. Doug's words came to mind: "tough as wet leather."
He looked to be in his late sixties or early seventies, but I suspected
he might be younger. He was repairing the clasp of a bracelet on a
woman's wrist, bowing over the counter to fix the chain.

"Since my dog bit me last Fourth of July, my hand has not
been right," he said, apologizing for his clumsiness. "I'm losing the
forward motion."

"Want me to hold one side?" the customer asked.

"I got it."

"There we go."

"That'll be $19.26. It will not break again."

The woman withdrew the bills from her purse.

"I thank you, ma'am. Have a blessed day."

He turned to me, hovering at the counter. I asked if he was
Moe Saunders, and he said he was. I told him that I had been talking to Doug in Rena Lara about a gentleman who'd lived down
there a few years, then moved to Clarksdale.

Moe squinted at me, as if trying to follow what I was saying or
remember who I was talking about.

"His name was Clinton," I said.

"Right, right," said Moe, his head bobbing. "Whatever happened to him? Clinton, Clinton . . ."

"You remember him?"

"Sure I remember him. Very interesting guy. Very interesting guy,"
he said, as if conjuring Clinton back to his mind through repetition.

"In what way?"

"He travelled all over. He could tie all sorts of knots. Just an interesting guy. I liked talking to him."

"Did he used to live here?"

"He did. Upstairs. Probably six months."

"Do you know why he left?"

"He may have been going on to Florida to visit his sister. Or his sister in Arkansas. He didn't talk too much about his family."

I nodded, waiting for him to continue.

"We just had numerous conversations, numerous. He worked for the zoo in California."

That was a new detail. "Did he know a lot about animals?" I asked, thinking about how Bax had made a living as a wilderness guide. His experiences with wildlife inspired his sculptures, which mostly feature big game.

"Right," Moe said. "He knew a lot about a lot of things." He padded his hand across the back of his neck. "Are you looking for him?"

"I've been here for a few days," I said. "Doing research. Doug in Rena Lara thought he had a few of his belongings. He suggested I come here and talk to you."

"I don't have any of his belongings," Moe said. "He stayed with a guy. Let me think of his name."

"Winston?"

"No. Winston's a good friend of mine. He stayed with a guy in town for three or four months, then he left again. He was talking about visiting his sister. Did he have a sister in Arkansas or one in Florida or something?"

"I think so," I said. "Do you know why he came here?"

"He was riding a bicycle down here, then he stopped in Rena Lara. He got arrested down there. Did you hear about that crazy—? They thought he was someone from, uh, New York or somewhere. They thought he killed someone, but they had the wrong person. He wasn't too happy about our sheriff's department here when they arrested him."

"How did he react?" I asked.

"He was pissed off. He wasn't the guy, but they kept him in jail. That's foolish. I would have been pissed off too."

I nodded.

"I don't know where in the— Let me see my friend across the street." He shuffled out from behind the counter and opened the front door, peered across the street at another business's window, one advertising harmonica lessons. "He's not there," Moe said. "Are you going to be in town for a few days?"

"I leave tomorrow, unfortunately."

"You looking for him?"

"Kind of . . ."

"Do you know how to get in touch with his sister?"

"Do you know her name?"

"No."

"Then no," I said, with a small laugh.

"Where you from?" Moe asked.

"Canada."

"Oh, Canada! See, the person he was supposed to have been was from Canada."

"Right," I said.

"Not New York. Canada. They arrested him here."

"Why'd they think it was him?"

"Looked like him, I guess. As far as I know, looked like him. He was riding his bicycle and his bicycle got stolen. We found his bicycle." Another detail I hadn't heard before. "I found it, and I pulled a gun on two guys and they dropped the bicycle."

I raised my eyebrows, reminded how collectively armed the people were down here, though I couldn't be sure what he told me was factual.

"He was tying all these fancy knots," Moe said again. "He was a very talented guy."

"Where's the bicycle now?"

"Oh, he left with it. I wish I could think of the guy's name, the guy he was staying with. Lived over here off Maple Street. He was an older guy. Walks with a cane and all. He was staying with him, the last I knew. Then he just up and just left. It's been almost a year ago probably."

"Do you know why he left? Did he say goodbye?"

"No. We kind of got into it 'cause he didn't clean up after himself. I told him, I'll help you out, but I ain't gonna wipe your ass."

"Fair enough."

"I wish I could tell you how to get in touch with him. I have no clue."

"We're here tomorrow morning. What time do you open?"

"Ten. I'll see if I can get the guy's name. You got a phone number I can call you?"

We had been using Jasmine's number, since she had an American phone plan. I wrote her first name and number on a scrap of till paper.

"I will get this guy's number," Moe said. "I'll tell this guy that y'all are looking for Clint."

"Thank you," I said. "I appreciate your willingness to help."

"Okay, well, I hope y'all find Clinton. He's really a good guy. He just needed a purpose. He just—almost like he wanted to disappear." I was surprised. It was the first time someone had worded this fact so simply. "He didn't want nobody to know where he was at," he went on.

"I wonder why," I said, hoping he might elaborate without my being too interrogative.

"He had no enemies," Moe said. "He was a wonderful guy. He had no enemies that I know of."

"Did he have a family?" I asked, meaning a wife, kids.

"He had a sister. We talked about numerous things. He was a real interesting guy to talk to. He lived up in Alaska for a number of years. His dad was in the military in California. I just remember vaguely, bits and pieces, about how he worked in the zoo and all."

I found it significant where the stories overlapped: The sister in Arkansas. From Alaska. Headed to Florida. Dad in the military. Convenient to be vague about where you grew up. Hard to fact-check, too, given his surname was so common.

"You have a blessed day," Moe said as I walked to the front door. "Y'all have a safe visit."

13.

SANDY

On our final morning in Mississippi, we met Doug's ex-wife, Sandy, at a restaurant called Rest Haven. Vinyl booths flanked one wall of the dining room; a serving counter lined with stools was on the other side. Sandy told us she would arrive in a "bad hair day hat," which I took to mean a hat due to a bad hair day, but sure enough, she arrived in a black tuque with the words *bad hair day* stitched in fuchsia. She was a wiry woman—no taller than five three, but tough-looking. I had no trouble imagining her as a labourer.

The server knew Sandy's order by heart: a Western omelet with every ingredient, grits, and a side of toast.

She launched into her story within minutes of sitting down, without preamble. If she perceived a bush, let's say she did not beat around it.

"I want to say it's been at least five years ago now," she told Jasmine and me as she stirred sugar into her coffee, the spoon chiming the sides of the mug. "I was questioning who he was. He and Doug would run off and get into these drug episodes. He was gone one day, so I went through his bags, and I found an ID that said Ronald Bax."

"Do you remember what kind of ID it was?" I asked.

"No. It was so long ago."

"You didn't take a photo of it, did you?"

"No. I looked him up online, though, because I was scared,"

she said. "I didn't expect him to come up right then. I actually got worried about myself after reading about what he had done. What I understood from Sheriff Jones was that his fingerprints didn't match. But oh my God, if you superimposed that picture over him, it was the exact same person."

I thought of Riley's words: *carbon copy*.

"The ages worked out, too," Sandy went on. "He was on a bicycle when he came through. He had no vehicle or anything like that. And it was just a photo identification card, not a driver's licence. I do remember that."

"So you went through, or you saw, his things," I started, tempering my words subconsciously, to avoid accusatory language.

"I went through his backpack."

"And were you expecting to find ID? Or something else?"

"I wanted to know if he was who he said he was."

"Right."

"I've always had—" She paused, as if considering how to word something. "My father's a minister," she said. "I've always had a good intuition. When I have a bad feeling about something, I'm generally right on cue with it."

I nodded.

"I didn't feel like he was telling us the truth about who he was, or where he came from."

"What made you feel that way?"

"I was creeped out. I don't know how to describe it. He gave me the heebies. And his story would change."

"Oh yeah?"

"Of course then I had a pretty good memory—it's going to hell lately—but his story would change about what he had done, where he had been. I'd question him on it. It was a lot of little things."

Before I could inquire about the inconsistencies, she returned to the day she went through his backpack. She spoke in a calm yet

non-linear manner: one anecdote tipping into another, many minutes passing before her story wended back to the original thread.

"It was the first opportunity I had to go through his stuff
because he never left his backpack. Somebody called, and he had to
run and meet them real quick. He left his backpack on the couch.
I knew I only had ten or fifteen minutes, so it was real quick.

"I looked at the name; I wrote it down in my book. I don't
know why I didn't take a picture of it—I was so hurried. I didn't
want him to catch me going through his stuff. Get me in trouble
for doing something that I felt, since he was in my home, I had a
right to do. But probably didn't, you know. And I see the name
Ronald Bax. That's when I looked him up. When his picture came
up, I fell out," she said, a genuine urgency in her voice. "I actually
got somebody else to look at the photo. She's passed on now. It was
my stepdaughter. She said, Oh my God, Sandy, that's him, it's got
to be him. I said, I agree, I think it is too."

There was so much information coming at once that I didn't
fully process that detail, that her stepdaughter had died. It was a
story we would return to.

I asked Sandy if she knew Riley, who worked at the Stone
Pony. She did, of course. Everyone knew everyone.

"She hadn't seen a photo of Ronald Bax," I said. "I showed
her, and she instantly recognized him as Clinton. She said it was
a carbon copy."

"It is. It's a carbon copy of him."

I glanced at Jasmine, beside me in the booth, listening carefully.

"Honestly, I've watched a lot of these shows," Sandy said. "I
know they can alter their fingerprints. They're not even sure if the
fingerprints they had on file, from what I read, are actually his prints."

"They are, I think. From the eighties. The old ink-and-roll ones."

"The eyes," Sandy said. "Oh my God, the eyes. Every feature.
The eyebrows. The age. Everything was spot-on."

"Do you remember what his hands looked like?"

"Well, he had smaller hands. He had a tattoo, though I couldn't begin to tell you where I wrote all that down. Everything I have is in storage right now. If I was to come across that, though, I'd tell you what the tattoo was. He had a tattoo on his arm, right here," she said, pointing to her upper arm. "Now I never saw any of this part." She traced her finger up her bicep to her shoulder. "It was uncanny, the resemblance," she said. "The shape of the chin. When I first met him, he had a very light moustache, but he started letting it go. It was carbon copy, that's all I can say. Carbon copy."

"I read in a newspaper article," I said, "and this may have been misquoted, but I read in a newspaper article that his hands appeared burned. Do you have any memory of that?"

"I don't have any memory of that, but there was a reason at the time. There was a reason I thought he had changed his finger-prints. That they wouldn't match. That they really needed to have someone talk to him, look at him."

"So even before the sheriff came, you thought he'd changed his fingerprints?"

"That's what I'm saying. Before they did that, I thought, well, his fingerprints won't match. I don't know why I thought that. Maybe it's because I did see a burn, but I don't remember."

She paused, as if searching again for her words, or a memory. "He was very . . . ," she started. "Even around our house, he wore gloves all the time."

"In your house?"

"In our house. You know those brown jersey gloves? He would work with my ex-husband. He never took those jersey gloves off. Even to sit down and to eat."

"Seriously?"

"It was strange things like that. Just strange. Eventually I left. I gave Doug an ultimatum."

"So they were getting into trouble, the two of them?" Jasmine asked.

"Yeah. I actually put my husband in jail the day after Thanksgiving." We must have looked alarmed, for Sandy laughed. "I'm very matter-of-fact."

"Well, if it's not a safe environment for you," I started.

"Yeah. I got my stuff, put it in storage, and moved into my parents'."

"Good for you," I said.

"I had a daughter. I couldn't have that around."

"She was living there too?"

Sandy nodded. "It blew my mind yesterday," she said, referring to our text message. "I hadn't thought of that in so long. I haven't seen him around town either. Somebody told me he moved to town, but I haven't seen him."

"He was living upstairs at Saunders Jewelry for six months," I said.

"That don't surprise me," Sandy said. "That's another dope-head in town."

"That's what we've heard."

"Sorry," she said. "I tell it like it is. Rena Lara is what you would call a good ol' boys' town. He would go and work for those guys. He wouldn't charge them a whole lot. So he became part of the good ol' boys' club. And when you're in the good ol' boys' club, no one believes you can do any wrong. Even for me," she went on. "My ex-husband laid his hands on me. That's why I got him arrested that day. We got into a fight, and he got physical. No one believed he laid hands on me. I got a black eye, my hand's pouring blood. They look right at me and say, Oh no, you did that to yourself."

The wider parallels struck me: violence, misogyny, lawlessness, isolation. I remembered what activist Lisa Tremblay had said about Whitehorse's undercurrents in 1992—that "many Yukoners believe Krystal deserved to die." Before this trip, a friend had warned me, "Don't underestimate small-town loyalty." I could see it here—but that loyalty was gendered.

"I went through the first husband like that," Sandy went on. "I wasn't going to do it again. I didn't see or hear anything of him for two and a half years, maybe three. Then I ran into my ex-husband, and he told me Clinton had moved to town."

I thought back to our conversations with Doug and Jonathan. I said, "You know, almost everyone we've talked to in Rena Lara has been a man. We've wondered if they've turned a blind eye to certain details."

"Most of them out there in the good ol' boys' club," Sandy said. "Most of them are criminals anyway. You can't really trust their judgment. I'm sorry," she said as the server arrived with our plates. "I truly believe it was him."

We slid our napkins and coffee cups out of the way to clear space.

"It was the best thing I did, moving away from there. They're all family. They're all my ex-husband's family."

"Right."

"I have a wonderful husband now," she told us. "He's an MRI technician out at the hospital."

"I'm happy for you," I said.

We fell into a food-welcoming silence, Sandy and Jasmine carving their omelets, me agitating a cloud of pepper onto my poached eggs.

"Do you remember any of the stories he would tell?" I asked. "The ones that didn't match up?"

"You know sometimes when somebody is telling an extravagance," she said.

"Yeah."

"Or . . . you ever met someone where everything you've done, they've done and done it better?"

"Sure," I said.

"That kind."

"Do you remember what he said he did for a living before he got to Rena Lara?"

"He probably told me, but to be honest I don't remember. I know he was biking across the country. He had a sister who held on to his money for him," she said. "I never believed it was actually a sister. I thought that maybe it was someone he trusted with his identity."

"Do you remember her name?"

"I don't, sorry. I didn't even think of the sister when I called CrimeStoppers. At the time, I was so upset at finding the identification, then finding the name online."

"So he was arrested," I said, returning to the timeline. "Then they kept him in jail for a few days . . ."

"Yeah, they kept him here. They ran his prints. Sheriff Jones said, I'm sorry, Sandy. They don't match. I said, You need to contact these people, because whether they match or not, I believe it's him." She continued: "He had his name. His belongings. Of course after he got arrested, he must have gotten rid of all that. Anything connected to that name. He didn't have his backpack on him anymore, so I'm assuming my ex-husband helped him on that one."

"Getting rid of the backpack?" I asked.

She nodded.

"Do you have any pictures of him?"

"I don't know," she said. "Maybe in storage. Let me go to my Facebook page and look at old photos."

We ate as she scrolled through her phone. After a few minutes, she shook her head and explained she would have to look on her husband's phone to find the older photos.

"That man gave me the willies," she said again. "I never even told my husband about him. I had to explain everything."

"Was that okay?" I asked, conscious that she was trying to keep her old life separate from her new one.

"Yeah," she said. "I said, honestly I haven't even thought of him since Sheriff Jones arrested him and let him go. I was looking at it this way—if it wasn't him, then he'd be exonerated, and I wouldn't have to worry about it. But everything in me," she said, and trailed off. "Even when they said no, the prints didn't match. Everything in me said it's gotta be. If Krystal was still alive today, she'd say yeah, it was him."

I stiffened, alarmed at her casual invocation of Krystal. We hadn't even discussed what Ronald Bax had done.

"She felt the same as I did," Sandy went on.

"Krystal . . . ?" I said, my heart thudding.

"My adopted daughter."

"Oh."

"I took her in when she was sixteen. She died when she was nineteen. She was with people she shouldn't have been with."

"I'm sorry, Sandy."

"I tried," she said. "It got to the point where she said, Okay, I'm moving out, Mom. I can't live here with this."

"Because of Clinton?" I asked. "The lifestyle he brought?"

"Right. At the time, my daughter from Florida had moved in with me also. She was sixteen. I had two girls. I wasn't going to risk anything happening to them."

We nodded, another quiet falling around our booth.

"Did Sheriff Jones take the ID?" I asked her.

"No," Sandy said. "Clinton told them he didn't have any identification. That's what I'm saying. They never found the identification. I'm the only one who saw that, and nobody believed me. That's how I got the name Ronald Bax. It didn't come out of thin air."

"Maybe he had ID that said Clinton Hill too," I said. "It's easy to get fake ID."

"I never saw it. Everybody paid him in cash. He said he was travelling and didn't have a chequing account, so he was able to get away with that."

She'd barely touched her omelet. She was being so gracious, answering our questions. I hoped she'd have a chance to eat.

"He was, what do you call it," she said. "A *transient*. That's what he dubbed himself. A transient. He said he'd been travelling from different states. He mentioned he had lived in Alaska. There were things that matched, but there were so many things that didn't. That's what made me question. I was scared to death to call the cops," she went on. "That they were gonna tell him who I was, that I called. They never released my name to him. They said a local Rena Lara woman had called. Of course, most people knew I was the bitch." She grinned at us. "They're the kind that settle it themselves. Not me. You cause something in my yard, I call the cops." She added, "I'm glad y'all are still looking into it."

"We're trying," I said.

"You all look into a lot of cases?"

"Not really," I said. "My interest in it . . . I knew somebody who knew the woman who was killed."

"I am so sorry," Sandy said, with genuine concern in her voice.

"She's not someone I knew personally. It happened when I was five years old."

"Well, I hope somebody can give you something to work with from here," Sandy said. "He could get lost in that small town because it was a code of everybody knew everybody and . . ."

"No law enforcement presence."

"Exactly. No law enforcement presence. That's where he's gonna go to next. He'll find a little place like that."

Sandy had thought her ex-husband was only smoking weed, she explained. After the divorce, his sister told her it was crystal meth. "I thought he was just drunk," she said. "When he started drinking, he couldn't stop. Him and Clinton both. They would drink a case, case and a half of beer in no time flat and be obliterated. Weed don't really bother me. It was the fact they would get so stupid."

"Did you ever talk to the Canadian police about Clinton?" I asked.

"No," Sandy said. "I called the helpline. CrimeStoppers."

Constable Thur had told us he spoke to Sandy. He had the dates recorded in his notes. Had she forgotten?

"From what I understand, they contacted the local sheriff. I told them I didn't want my name released. But I knew Sheriff Jones, so I went and talked to him after they let Clinton go." She prodded her grits, which had congealed into a waxy mass on her plate. "I worried he was going to come after me," she said. "But he knew I had two nine millimetres. I never went anywhere without my gun on my side. Regularly, I would set up my target and shoot. He knew I was a dead-on bull's-eye. I made sure he knew that.

"There used to be a little store in Rena Lara," she went on. "A little red building, where everyone would sit out on the porch every evening. Used to be called Rico's."

That's the place Walt had mentioned.

"That's where they'd hang out," she said. "Drink, talk. Nobody said anything about him living behind the levee?"

"He lived behind the levee?"

"At one time. He lived in a trailer. Winston Kelly's trailer."

"Oh, that did come up. The name Winston."

"He used to live in Winston's trailer for a while. I don't know what dates. That might have been right before he moved to town. He could still be there, for all I know."

"I don't think so," I said. "Everyone we've talked to said they haven't seen him in a long time."

"Which people?"

I hesitated. We hadn't told Sandy that we'd visited her former husband.

"Rena Lara people?" she asked.

"Rena Lara people."

"Still wouldn't surprise me," she said.

"Is there another Clinton?" Jasmine asked. "In Rena Lara?"

"Not that I'm aware of."

"Do you think your ex-husband would hide him for any reason?"

"Oh, definitely," Sandy said. "They truly believe he was just Clinton."

"Right."

"Doug, for all intents and purposes," Sandy said, "he's a dope-head. But he has a good heart. When he befriends someone like that, he'll protect them and take care of them. He's always been like that. He's got his bad points, but he's got his good points. Just, his bad points outweighed his good points."

"Do you have a cordial relationship with him?" Jasmine asked.

"I'd say cordial. We talk now and then. I avoid him if possible. I got rid of that part of my life. He always calls me about needing work. I tried to help him a couple times but that backfired on me."

"When we talked to Doug," Jasmine said, "he mentioned a Clint. I got the impression there was another Clinton in the area. Or even within . . . I know his property stretches . . . I don't know how far. He mentioned another Clint 'out back.'"

"No," Sandy said. "If he's talking about a Clint, he's talking about *that Clint*."

"I know what you're talking about," I cut in, reluctant to jump to this, radical to me, conclusion: that Clinton had been in town, indeed "out back" from Doug's house, the whole time we were there. "I think there's another guy who lives there named Clinton."

"Girl," Jasmine said, "I don't know."

"No, I'm telling you," Sandy said. "There is not another Clinton around that area. I know his family."

"Then why did Doug have his things in the shed?" I asked. "He implied there was another individual staying in a trailer nearby who had the name Clinton."

"No." Sandy said it so bluntly, I released a fluttering laugh. "Okay."

"I'm sorry, honey," she said. "No."

"What if they're covering for him?" Jasmine asked.

"They would, that's what I'm saying," said Sandy. "After the fingerprint deal, they never believed that was him."

"She's talking about this good ol' boy system," Jasmine said. "And if they have a relationship where they're partying, and they're good friends."

"Yeah. If he said Clint out back, it's Clint out back."

"How would we find out if he's still there?" Jasmine asked.

"I don't know," Sandy said. "I guess I could always pop over for a visit. Say I'm coming to look for a . . ." She hunted for an item she might feasibly seek. "Tub."

We laughed.

"God, I wish I could remember the address of Winston's trailer," Sandy said. "Do you have a pen? I'll draw y'all a map." She dug a paint swatch from her purse and began to sketch on it. She directed us, on the map, over the levee, over a bend, another bend, then another. Then a sharp turn at a wood shanty. And right next to it, there would be a trailer, she told us. On a hill.

"From what I gathered," Jasmine said, "he really made himself at home here. In a way he wouldn't want to leave."

"He inserted himself as a member of the community out there," Sandy agreed. "Anybody needed help, he'd help. The personality he'd flip forward. But I've seen Clinton drunk and with a temper. I saw things others didn't."

"You saw his temper?" I said.

"Uh-huh. And could he be capable of it? Oh yes."

"Do you think there's a chance," Jasmine asked, "he left awhile and now he's back?"

"That's a good possibility," Sandy said. "If Clinton felt threatened by anything, he wouldn't even go to the grocery store. With Rico's being closed out there now, if it is, people aren't going to see him. That was the only place he felt comfortable to go. He wouldn't even go to the Country Store to hang out, and they got pool tables and stuff. He'd sit outside at the other store. Maybe he's living in the shed now."

"We saw the shed next to the house," I said.

"No, that's the barn. There's another shed behind the house. It's very small."

"Doug mentioned it," I said, remembering now. "But he didn't show us."

"'Out back' could also refer to behind the levee," Sandy said. "Yeah, he's still there. He's staying out in Winston's old house. I know exactly where he is. He could have been in the other bedroom while you were there. He could have listened to everything y'all said."

Another flutter of laughter.

"I'm telling you ladies, it's him."

I was still trying to replay the scene, what Doug said the moment we walked into his house. It was before I started recording. He and Brooke had both referred to a Clinton out back, but I couldn't remember who said what first. I kicked myself for not recording as we walked through the door, but I'd wanted to ask permission.

"I always get a vibe from people," Sandy said. "From the moment I laid eyes on him, that vibe came and never left. No matter how much he convinced everybody else. I don't care how many dishes he washed for me . . . that's the way I felt about him."

She paused. "Wait, where did y'all meet him?"

"Well, we . . . Jonathan, who also goes by Worm—"

"Yes, I love Worm."

"Riley put us in touch with him and he drove us to Doug's house."

"Was it on Highway 1, do you remember?"

"Yes."

"Damn it, y'all, Clinton was there. Y'all need to not ever, *ever*— let me go ahead and tell you—from now on, don't meet anyone in their home. Let this be a lesson. Make them meet you in a public place, because y'all, he was there. Two strange people coming up— did y'all talk to Doug on the phone about what you were coming to talk to him about?"

"We were careful what we said to him," I said.

"I wonder if Worm told him you were on your way."

"Worm did text him," I said.

"Worm probably told Doug why y'all were coming and if Clinton was there, he sent him out back. He would have hid in the shed."

"It's just weird that he then said, Oh yeah, Clint, Clint out back. Unless he was being sloppy."

"No, that's him," Sandy said. "Trust me. I was married to him. If he said 'out back, I'll go and get him,' he's in the shed hiding. He probably said, 'Let me see what's up. Jonathan texted, they're on their way here. Go out there and let me see what's up. When they leave I'll let you know.' *This* is Doug," she said. "God, it's so horrible. I'm freaking out about what y'all could have went through."

It seemed far-fetched to me. Yet Sandy would know how many Clintons lived in town. She would know how her ex-husband described his friend, or what he might do in this situation. Wouldn't she?

"Ironically," said Jasmine, "the woman Ron Bax did kill, her name was Krystal."

"Well, I know he was nowhere near where Krystal was. She was gang-raped and shot up with heroin," Sandy said.

The cruelty of this information silenced me.

"Walt called me at four o'clock in the morning. I'll never forget that. She wasn't my blood child but she was my child."

"When did that happen?"

"Four years ago now."

"So that whole stint of time for you . . . ," said Jasmine.

"It was rough. I went through so much in that time frame. I left Doug. I moved into this house in town. She had promised me—she had been taking pain pills. She went to get pain pills, ironically for Doug's sister. Some Xanax. She went by herself, an apartment with several men. They shot her up with what they call black . . ."

"Black tar?" said Jasmine.

"Black tar heroin," Sandy said. "And they found her body. One of Doug's cousins was involved. She was soaking wet. They took pictures of her, made fun of her being drunk and passed out. I didn't realize at the time when I looked at the pictures from two in the morning—she was already dead. That's another one of those good ol' boys cover-ups out there."

I was crushed hearing these details. The thought of those boys on their joyride while this nineteen-year-old girl was dead or dying. Did they know? The story still leaves a pit in my stomach. I've tried to find this Krystal (or Kristal or Crystal—I don't know how she spelled her name): a news article, an obituary, some trace of her. I haven't found a thing. This was one of those moments where the preoccupation that sent this book into motion—a woman killed, justice unresolved—repeated on me with unsparing sharpness. I thought of Elizabeth Hanson's 2012 article for the *Yukon News*: "twenty years on, I wonder if we have learned anything from the countless Krystals who have died in this country . . ."

And now, Sandy's stepdaughter, Krystal. The echo felt too obvious—almost garish.

"Did they go to jail?" I asked.

"No one went to jail. Like I said, it's a good ol' boys' club. Depends on who you know."

Eventually, the conversation returned to Doug and Clinton. Sandy described how Clinton looked the last time she'd seen him: skinny, climbing a hill on his bicycle. She said he'd lost weight due to the drugs. "He looked like death warmed over."

The server brought a box for Sandy's breakfast, which she'd still barely touched.

"You ladies be careful," Sandy added. "Don't go to anybody else's home. Don't ride with anybody else. Always meet on a neutral ground."

"We've been pretty safe," Jasmine said. "Worm took us over to Doug's house."

"But in retrospect, you hadn't met Worm either."

"True," I said.

"He could have been leading you to slaughter. Maybe that's my mistrustful side," she said. "But I promise you, one of them snapped a picture of y'all just to show him. So be careful."

14.

AWAKEDNESS

Our bodies hummed as we left Rest Haven. I was shaken by the possibility that Clinton had been on the property during our visit with Doug—that he'd overheard our conversation. That notion felt so wild to me, I struggled to accept it, especially if Clinton had anything to do with Ronald Bax. My mind traced back to other conversations we'd had: Worm's certainty that Clinton was in Arkansas, which was minutes across the state border—"I'd bet a hundred— I'm a hundred percent sure." Brooke's offer to go get him. Her silence when Doug said it was a different Clinton. Sandy's own conviction. I was feeling overwhelmed.

We drove home the long way, past Saunders Jewelry, and stopped in to see if Moe had been able to reach his friend, the guy Clinton had last stayed with. He hadn't, but there were two moments of note.

First, he pegged Jasmine with his gaze, stated her first and last name, which we hadn't told anyone, and said she lived in Houston, Texas, a detail we hadn't told Moe. This unnerved us both. He said the information had come up when he Google-searched her phone number. I felt terrible—and stupid—that we'd used her real number.

The second moment occurred as we were leaving the store. We had paused in front of the doorway, turning to Moe to say goodbye.

"Right there," Moe said. "I remember Clint standing right

there. I snapped a picture of him. Boy, he got so mad. He made me delete it from my phone."

"He didn't like his photo being taken?" I asked.

"He hated it."

I wondered why, if Clinton wasn't hiding from anything. It's one thing to be camera shy. It's another to get angry and make your friend delete photos of you from their phone.

We drove one last circle around Clarksdale to snap final photographs. We were pulling up to our Airbnb, to load our suitcases, when the tire blew. Jasmine had been so preoccupied with the morning as well—our conversation with Sandy, our parting words with Moe—that she drove into the curb. We had to be at the Memphis airport in a matter of hours. As chance would have it, the tire blew within a few hundred metres of a Firestone. The Jeep crawled the distance, barely making it up the parking lot slope. After we replaced the tire, and later, pulled into a body shop to get the rims painted so Avis wouldn't notice, Sandy called.

I put her on speaker. She and her father were preparing to leave for Memphis in advance of her father's medical appointment when her dad had spotted Winston down the road from the police station.

"He said, I think that's Winston sitting down there in that parking lot," she told us. "I said, I don't know. He said, Don't you think that looks like him? I said, Well, I think so, but I'm not sure. Then we watched as the county constable met with him. As we drove back, I was able to see into the vehicle. It *was* Winston." They'd talked for twenty or thirty minutes, she told me.

"Huh," I said. "Do you have any idea why Winston would be talking to the constable?"

"None. And like I said, it's strange that he's doing it the day after you talked to Doug, in a parking lot away from the police station. He had to pass the police station to come to the parking lot.

I thought it was strange," she repeated. "Winston of all people is meeting with the county constable."

"Because he wouldn't normally talk to law enforcement?"

"No," she laughed. "He's as big of a dopehead and dealer as the rest of them. So talking to the constable—if anything he'd be running from them."

"This is weird, Sandy."

"It really is. One thing's for sure—you guys have opened an awakedness out there that has made several people aware of the situation, whereas I was too scared of the consequences."

"Do you think that's a problem for people out there? Or for you? Or for anybody?"

"No. I just never talked with anyone out there about it, because I was too scared with him being within reaching distance of me. I couldn't say for damn sure one way or another, is this the guy who murdered. Yes, he had the ID. Did he steal it? I don't know. Does he look exactly like him? Yes. Does everything tell me it's him? Yes. So I wasn't going to start spreading rumours. You know how small towns are."

"So I wonder if he *was* staying at one of Winston's trailers," I said.

"I guarantee he was. I'd be willing to bet money on it."

My first impression of Sandy: I trusted her. Why would she lie about the information card years later, and years after her divorce? Come 2015, when she called CrimeStoppers, Ronald Bax's name hadn't been in the media for twenty years—not since 1995, when *Unsolved Mysteries* aired that ninety-second clip. After the show's host, Robert Stack, died in 2003, they played reruns in syndication until the contracts with Lifetime and Spike TV ended in 2008 and 2010 respectively. The show began streaming on Amazon Prime and Hulu in 2017, but it was not broadcast or available for streaming between 2010 and 2017, the period when everything unfolded between Sandy, Doug, and Clinton Hill.

How could Sandy land on Ronald Bax, of all wanted men in North America, to pin an identity on her ex-husband's lodger? To find someone who bore such striking resemblance, according to everyone who saw him, who was of the same age and height, who came from the same region—the chances were remote. Yet I didn't trust myself to dispute the conclusions of an FBI analyst and an RCMP investigator.

The day after our conversation, Sandy learned her dad had to have a heart bypass. Our exchanges slowed as she focused on caring for him. I followed up with Moe and attempted to call the person who had last lived with Clinton in town. The former roommate said, "I don't even know who you are," and hung up. I noticed a theme: in person, people were helpful, but southern hospitality did not extend to the phone. I did contact Riley shortly after I flew home. I asked if she or her husband knew anyone else in Rena Lara named Clinton. She said they did not.

From Montreal, I sent the RCMP in Whitehorse an email summarizing my findings: that an individual had arrived in Rena Lara by bicycle between 2011 and 2013. That he'd taken a ferry from Alaska to Washington State and was endeavouring to cycle to Florida. That he stopped by Rena Lara to ask for directions to a campsite, and a resident offered a place to stay. That he did not have government-issued ID but he secured under-the-table work in kitchens, at local farms, as well as by cutting trees. That he had a "sister in Arkansas," who allegedly brought him credit cards and wired him money. That the wife of the Rena Lara resident didn't believe his stories, and when she went through his backpack, she found an information card with the name Ronald Jeffrey Bax. That when I showed a photo of Bax to a local bartender, who remembered the individual as a patron, she reacted with visible recognition, saying it looked like a carbon copy of the guy. Just older, his hairline receded. That I came home with a few items that may have belonged to him, and I'd be happy to mail them in case they could be tested for DNA evidence.

I addressed my memo to the division's Major Crime Unit and sent it to the strategic communications director, the only contact we had aside from Const. Craig Thur. I cc'd Thur for good measure, though he hadn't been on the case for two years. I didn't expect to hear from him, yet it was Thur who replied within one business day.

He asked me to expand on why I believed the bicycle helmet, sweater, and cell phone could belong to Clinton Hill, as well as whether they'd been stored in dry conditions. He said they were willing to receive these items, but it would help to know more about their "potential probative value."

He also shared what he knew about the Mississippi tip:

On Monday, March 9th, 2015 Clinton HILL was fingerprinted at the Coahoma County Sheriff's office in Clarksdale Mississippi.

On Tuesday, March 10th, 2015 the Federal Bureau of Investigation identified the fingerprints to an individual already in their database. They were not the fingerprints of Ronald BAX. I continued to pursue this possible lead.

On Wednesday, March 11th, 2015 I spoke with [the *Press Register* journalist] followed by a lengthy conversation with Sandy CUSSEN. During these conversations I made detailed notes.

At no time did Sandy CUSSEN mention to me that she or her friend ever found identification or an information card "bearing the name Ronald Jeffrey BAX." I clearly remember Sandy CUSSEN being intent in trying to convince me that Clinton HILL was Ronald Jeffrey BAX. I therefore find it perplexing that this card was not mentioned. It would not likely have been something Sandy would have forgotten.

I, too, found Sandy's omission of the information card perplexing. Based on our conversations with Sandy, Doug, and the *Press Register* journalist, I understood that she found the card several months before she reported it—no later than Thanksgiving 2014, when she moved into her parents' house. Did the time that lapsed between November and March blur what she deemed important to tell Thur? Or was she lying to us? I had been in touch with Sandy over the subsequent months, but she never replied to my last messages asking if we could speak on the phone. Given the global pandemic, and her unwell father, I wasn't surprised—but it presented a wall. I was left with my own obsessive wondering—my mind tracking over and over the same questions.

Did Bax have a doppelgänger? Everyone in Rena Lara said Clinton Hill looked just like the guy in the wanted poster—even those trying to defend Clinton, like Jonathan and Doug. My mind returned to Riley, who had no skin in the game whatsoever. She had visibly gasped when I showed her Bax's photo. Even their heights matched—shorter than average for a man. Often people in Whitehorse described Bax as "not a big guy." Similarly, Doug mentioned several times how "little" Hill was. Five seven, the height listed by the RCMP, would surely appear "little" to someone who was six feet. However, without seeing Clinton Hill for ourselves, we can't take his physical resemblance to Bax for granted. Constable Thur told me, when we spoke on the phone for the first time in December 2020, that he wasn't convinced.

"Just looking at a photograph of Terry Clinton Hill and looking at a photograph of Ronald Bax, I don't think they're the same person," Thur said. "Ronald Bax was a pretty good-looking guy. And Clinton Hill is not a very good-looking guy. Now I realize that all those years have gone by, and people live hard, but I don't think it's him."

At the very least, their height and age matched. It was also a striking coincidence that this person travelled from the same area where Krystal was killed by a mode of transport inherently under the radar, with no ID or apparent personal attachments except a sister who wired him money every week. Striking coincidences do happen. But what about the tattoo? Two people (Riley's husband and Sandy) claimed to have seen Bax's winged horse tattoo, though it's possible they embellished this memory, or absorbed the detail after reading the RCMP wanted ad. Human brains can be unreliable and spongy. While Thur had directed the sheriffs to inspect the areas of Hill's body where Bax had tattoos, they only received this instruction after Hill was released. They couldn't bring him in again after he was cleared, so no one ever checked Hill for tattoos.

Thur acknowledged that it wasn't impossible that Bax had assumed Hill's identity, but he found it highly improbable. "He had a northern accent, well, Terry Clinton Hill was from Oregon. And all these other things, right. But I'm really skeptical he had a card on him that said Ron Bax, because I would not have ignored that or not remembered that if I heard that when I spoke to the people I spoke to over the phone in 2015. No one mentioned that to me."

"That continues to confuse me," I replied. "You spoke to the journalist in Clarksdale. The detail about the ID was mentioned in the article she wrote that same week. That's how I got wind of it."

A faintly uncomfortable silence stretched between us.

"Yeah. I don't know. I don't know how to explain that."

Part of me wondered if Sandy had assumed Thur already

knew about the information card—that that was the premise of his call. It was the journalist who had phoned the RCMP, not Sandy, and the journalist who had passed on Sandy's number. Sandy had confided in the journalist about the card a few days earlier. Did she figure Thur was up to speed? According to Thur, the journalist didn't mention the information card either, but she did highlight it in her newspaper article, published the same week. Could it be put down to a miscommunication?

Or did Sandy invent the information card altogether? If so, why? To avenge her husband? To find leverage in their divorce? That's certainly what the good ol' boys would think. But if she fabricated the story, how did she find a look-alike (if they did look alike, as the residents of Rena Lara remember)? Why retell this story ardently, four years later? Why meet with us at all? Why then call us after our meeting to report that Winston was talking to the county constable?

But also: Why not return my calls? Because she grew tired of thinking about this, or because her father was unwell? How would Sandy explain the inconsistencies?

After my phone conversation with Constable Thur, I was left with more questions than answers. We exchanged a few more emails in early 2021, and he emailed a contact in Washington, DC, to check the full arrest history of Terry Clinton Hill, which hadn't been included in the original files sent to Whitehorse from Rena Lara. An FBI agent on the West Coast confirmed that Hill was arrested in 1980, twelve years before Krystal's murder, and again in February 1992, a month before Krystal's murder. Thur didn't share the charges. The fingerprints taken in Clarksdale in 2015 match the prints from 1980 and 1992.

"The arrest history of someone is not normally something I would share," Thur told me over email. "However, I feel it is important that the truth of the matter is that Ronald BAX does not

appear to be living in the United States under the name Terry Clinton
HILL. The evidence is that they are two separate individuals."

When the FBI agent asked Thur if he wanted the known images
of Bax compared with those of Hill, Thur took him up on it. He
received a Report of Examination from the FBI's Digital Evidence
Laboratory in May 2021. It stated: "A facial comparison was conducted between HILL and BAX. Multiple differences in class and
distinguishing characteristics were observed between the individuals. Due to observed differences, HILL does not appear to be BAX."

It felt strange, knowing this for a fact. I had grown comfortable
in the permissive space of uncertainty. Jasmine and I had travelled
to Rena Lara expecting to find nothing. What we found exceeded
our imaginations. It's hard to unstitch my preoccupation with that.
At times, this case has felt like a maze with the centre locked on
all sides. In the absence of Krystal and Ronald Bax, I followed
the threads that continued to generate doorways. Flinging myself
through each opening until I reached another dead end. That's
why I went to Mississippi in the first place: of all the fragments we
were left with, this one kept producing new threads. The cumula-
tion of coincidences remains impressive and puzzling to me, but
the more I learn about criminal investigations, the more I understand that coincidences are rife and not necessarily meaningful.

As for Clinton's items—while the investigator now managing
Krystal's case had accepted them in spring 2020, they couldn't test
them then, due to lab delays caused by COVID-19. A year and a
half later, the box was mailed back to me unopened.

Part of me still wonders, stubbornly: What if? What if Sandy
is telling the truth? Thur's findings rule out the possibility that
Clinton Hill is Ronald Bax, but they don't totally rule out the chance
that Sandy found an information card in Bax's name. They don't
rule out the possibility—however remote it may be—that Hill's
path crossed with Bax's in Alaska. It's unlikely. Yet, as credulous

as it sounds to say so, I still trust Sandy. Even if she invented the information card, I imagine it crystallized a truth for her: that this man living with them was hiding something, or from something. I was left wanting to know more about Ronald Bax: who he was, and where he was, if he was still alive.

An undated press release for Bax's limited-edition bronze sculptures describes him as an "established member of the Yukon Art Society," a "professional taxidermist, whose work is displayed throughout Canada and the United States," and "a recognized contributor to community art pieces," which include a flock of snowbirds for Yukon College, the bronze seal for the City of Whitehorse, previously mounted at city hall, and the Village Monument at Haines Junction.

While local carpenters constructed the base of the Haines Junction monument, Bax collaborated with sculptor and taxidermist Chuck Buchanan on the top: a snow-capped mountain with various emerging wildlife. The monument's round base, with narrow vertical planks that resemble a cupcake paper, has inspired locals to nickname the monument "the Muffin." Creatures protrude from the muffin top, including a bear, a moose, a Dall sheep, a wolf, and a mountaineer with binoculars, all built from the same foam used in taxidermy.

The press release continues, "Ron's experience as an outfitter's guide is a fundamental component to creating sculpting that depicts Canada's big game animals in a natural setting. Capturing the game as spotted in the wild, Ron takes pride in offering public and private collectors a piece of the Canadian wild through the medium of bronze sculpting."

A friend of Ron's had owned two of his polar bear pieces, "big ones," about the size of small dogs. "You could put them right on the floor and it almost looked like they were walking along," he recalled. "The one I gave my parents, my little brother came visiting with their Jack Russell dog, and that frigging thing came in the door, saw the bear, and attacked it. The fact that it had a power to it. It looked alive."

Within a week of Krystal Senyk's murder, all of Bax's art on the market had sold. Disrepute can be lucrative.

Myles and I met Mike,[1] another friend of Ron's, on my trip to the Yukon in 2018. He didn't want to meet in a public place where someone might overhear our conversation. Nor did he want to meet at his home. He directed us to Fish Lake Road in Porter Creek, where he was waiting in his Jeep. We conducted the interview between our vehicles, Mike glancing over his shoulder every time a car trundled past.

Mike had moved to the territory from Toronto in 1982. He'd met Ron in a bar, and they ended up living together in a trailer at Paddlewheel Village. He remembers Nick Cannell—later suspected, and cleared, of helping Bax escape—as Bax's best friend at the time. Mike and Ron shared common interests, including hiking and photography. They would visit a game farm owned by another friend, Mike snapping photos of the animals, Bax building sculptures from the images.

Ron was a private person, Mike said—"he'd be open one minute, shut down the next." Several times, he referred to Ron as "strange" or "offside," yet he knew no one better in the outdoors. "You could tell when you went out with him," he said. Mike had taken a few survival courses—he thought he knew his stuff—but Ron rivalled even his teachers. "An eight or nine out of ten," Mike said, assessing himself as a five.

Ron owned at least ten guns, some of them worth $1,200. The hunters he guided on expeditions would leave them as tips.

After the murder, police searched Mike's house. He warned the investigators that Ron was going to disappear. He could hike across the border, trail or no trail, he said; "he was an animal out there in the wilderness." And he was an excellent shot.

When we asked Mike where he thought Ron might be now, he suggested South America; Ron had a client and friend down there who bought his art. We told him the RCMP's theory, that there was a 70 percent chance Ron had committed suicide.

"No way he killed himself," Mike said. "Not a chance in hell." He said Ron was too proud and arrogant—not self-pitying.

Mike described some other sides of Ron, such as one time when he gave a married woman flowers. He knew she was married, but that didn't deter him. Mike was friends with the woman's husband, who eventually confronted Ron at the local bar. "Watch his hands," Mike had cautioned his friend before the altercation. "He's always prepared for the bush."

A few others described Bax as a Lothario. A local from Carcross, whose daughter used to babysit for Colleen and Ron's boys, used the word "brash" to describe all three of them: Ron, Colleen, and Krystal. However, Ron received special mention as a "redneck macho blond asshole who thought he was God's gift to women."

Another friend of Ron's remembered that Ron blamed Krystal for his marital strife. He used to refer to her and Colleen as "cunt-slappers." Ron had surveilled Krystal's house "spot and scope," according to this friend, and talked about "'ventilating' her house—.30-06 ventilation," a reference to a rifle cartridge. "But that was as close as he came to saying, 'I'm going to shoot the bitch,'" the friend added. "That's what the cops wanted me to say—that he premeditated it. It was major premeditated. At the same time, I could not say that he said he was going to kill her."

On whether or not he thought Ron had killed himself, this friend suggested it could have gone either way. "Fifty-fifty he's in the wind, or he's lying underneath a big boulder in some old den, right, where he crawled in and shot himself. Just sad, sad, sad, sad."

Another former friend, Robin, met Ron in the early eighties when he first moved to the Yukon. They "chummed around" and grew close over the years. Then in the mid-eighties Robin moved for work and Ron got married. They drifted apart. When Robin moved back to the area, they'd get together now and then for a cup of coffee.

Robin described Ron as friendly and gregarious, into the outdoors and hunting, as well as taxidermy and art. He never saw Ron's personality shift, and this perplexed him after the murder. Ron had come to his place that morning for coffee. They shot the breeze, then Ron left. Robin knew he was going through a divorce, that it wasn't pretty, but he had no idea how bad.

Unlike Mike, Robin *could* imagine his friend hiking into the bush "to do himself in." But equally, he knew Ron could survive for months on his own, that "you could easily cross the border and go from there."

April 13 / 95 —

3 years have gone. Time it is said heals all. This to some people might be true but to others not so. Time has changed nothing. When a life has been taken by a person for whatever reason, people who take other people's lives in our society pay very little for their crime. I have a picture of you in my room. Every day without missing a day, morning and before I go to bed, I give you a kiss in hopes that in the heaven of all men and women you are at one with the Lord. I have said this before but it is on my mind – the fear of dying by Ron Bax in your house, where a person is supposed to be safe, runs through my mind when I open my door.

I visit you each time I come to the Yukon, at least twice a day. My life has changed along with my mother, Uncle P—, Aunt S— and Aunt T—.

I am still working with Rick Noack RCMP Whitehorse. We will all talk about you on your birthday and one day Bax will be caught. Then everyone will try to get him off. I wanted to put something happy down but you are 33 and I am 57. You are always on my mind Krystal.

Love,

Dad   xxxxxxx

oooooooo

15.

WHO STAYS SAFE

A damsel must be white. This requirement is non-negotiable. It helps if her frame is of dimensions that breathless cable television reporters can credibly describe as "petite," and it also helps if she's the kind of woman who wouldn't really mind being called "petite," a woman with a good deal of princess in her personality. She must be attractive—also nonnegotiable. Her economic status should be middle class or higher, but an exception can be made in the case of wartime.

—Eugene Robinson, "(White) Women We Love,"
Washington Post (June 10, 2005)

As I prepared to write this book, and ingested primarily true crime content for five years, the damsel rhetoric around white female murder victims started to disturb me. For instance, the 2016 investigative podcast *Up and Vanished*, hosted by Payne Lindsey: "Tara Grinstead was a thirty-year-old former beauty queen and local high school teacher living in the small town of Ocilla, Georgia," the voiceover opens. "She was a gorgeous brunette with a striking smile and someone her students and peers looked up to."[1] I was engrossed in this podcast. Also, I wondered: What did Grinstead's beauty, or her smile, have to do with it?

I felt a similar cringe while reading Sharon Butala's *The Girl in Saskatoon*, which follows the murder of twenty-three-year-old Alexandra Wiwcharuk, found on the banks of the Saskatchewan River in 1962. From the first page: "The girl—or more properly, a young woman—dark, small, and exquisitely pretty, appears lost in her thoughts."[2]

Then there was the fanatic coverage of fourteen-year-old Elizabeth Smart, who was abducted from her bed in 2002 and found alive nine months later. *People* magazine named Smart one of the "50 Most Beautiful People" in 2005, alongside Julia Roberts, Halle Berry, and Angelina Jolie. "Most Beautiful Rising Star," the headline specified. Smart's father stated it was nice for his daughter to make the news for something other than kidnapping.[3]

John Berger says it simply: "men act;" "women appear."[4]

Specifically, white women. Conventionally attractive, middle-class white women appear. Even—especially—in their disappearance.

Krystal Senyk was not a damsel. Krystal built her own home. She hunted grizzly bears. She competed in international arm wrestling contests. Yet I question whether her murder would have received the same media attention or manhunt in the Yukon had she been Indigenous. To write of homicide in this country—especially in the Yukon, where in 2016 Indigenous people made up 23 percent of the population (compared with 5 percent in Canada overall)—it's necessary to confront the reality of what violence we talk about and what violence we turn away from.

According to the Canadian Femicide Observatory, Indigenous women are twelve times more likely to be murdered or missing than other women in Canada and sixteen times more likely than white women—a disparity so jarring it speaks for itself.[5] In 2020, 28 percent of all homicide victims in Canada were First Nations, Métis, or Inuit, with men accounting for over 80 percent of this number.[6] Indigenous people are also ten times more likely than white people to be killed by police.[7]

Statistics themselves are problematic. In 2020, 201 homicide victims were Indigenous,[8] but that number cleans, objectifies, numbs, and compresses the reality of those lives, 201 of them, and everyone who grieves them. An individual's humanity and uniqueness get lost in a number, as well as in phrases like "missing and murdered Indigenous women and girls." However, it's necessary to consider these numbers, because of what they reveal: that you're most likely to be killed in Canada if you're Indigenous.

Whereas violence against Indigenous men remains largely undiscussed, the murders of Indigenous women and girls have received broad public treatment in the past decade. Researcher Kristen Gilchrist published an article on the subject in 2010, four years before the murder of Tina Fontaine captured national attention and six before the government of Canada launched the National Inquiry into Missing and Murdered Indigenous Women and Girls. However, the findings in Gilchrist's article remain devastatingly pertinent.

News organizations judge every day what constitutes a valuable (read: clickable) crime or victim, and these decisions filter through a dominantly Western, white, heteronormative, middle-class, and often male lens. First, a story is worth telling if it occurred "nearby." Viruses do not disturb us until they enter local airports. Murders do not disturb us unless they're on our street—and if we live on a long street, if the victim resembles us, or our daughter, or our friend. Shock value is important. Violence disturbs us less if it's "ordinary," such as violence in the home, or by people who know each other, or people leading "high-risk" lifestyles, whom we expect to meet violent ends.

Bodies matter. From art to film to literature to news, the white female body has come to model purity and innocence. By contrast, the media has devalued non-white bodies. Often they're not even seen, or they're seen as perpetrators. Similarly, if a victim deviates from social patriarchal norms, such as by drinking or using substances, or dressing "provocatively," or walking on her own, or having sex, or having sex for money, the narrative pivots to blame her.

Gilchrist's article compares the media coverage of the disappearances and murders of three Indigenous women from Saskatchewan—Daleen Bosse, 26, Melanie Geddes, 24, and Amber Redman, 19—with the disappearances and murders of three white women from Ontario—Ardeth Wood, 27, Alicia Ross, 25, and Jennifer Teague, 18. Four of the women—Amber Redman, Melanie Geddes, Alicia Ross, and Jennifer Teague—disappeared within the same seven-week period in 2005. All six worked or attended school, and all had been close with their families.[9]

When Gilchrist counted the number of articles in local press that mentioned these cases, she found the white women were named 511 times, compared with 82 times for the Indigenous women. Gilchrist further filtered the articles to include only those that discussed the women's specific cases, finding 187 articles about the white women, compared with 53 about the Indigenous women. Tallying the number of words published in each article, Gilchrist found 135,249 words written for the white women, compared with 28,493 for the Indigenous women—nearly five times fewer. More than a third (37 percent) of the articles about the disappeared white women appeared on the front page, versus 25 percent of the articles on the Indigenous women; articles about the Indigenous women tended to be "hidden amongst advertisements," Gilchrist noticed, with more prominence given to soft news items, such as an article about an October snowfall. Below it, a picture of two geese in the road, captioned "A little off course."

In addition to her quantitative analysis, Gilchrist undertook a qualitative assessment of the articles, finding that headlines referred to the three Indigenous women impersonally and rarely by name. For example: "RCMP Identifies *Woman*'s Remains," or "*Teen*'s Family Keeping Vigil" (emphasis my own), compared with the missing white women, who were invoked by first and last names, even nicknames. For white women, the editors composed headlines as personal messages from the victims' friends and family, such as, "Jenny We Love You, We Miss You," or "Waiting for Alicia." Gilchrist further notes that the white women were described with beaming adjectives such as "devout," "so beautiful," "cherished," "a lily among the thorns," having "a luminous smile." Drier adjectives described the Indigenous women, who were "shy," "nice," "educated," "a good mom"—and these words were not bolstered by personal anecdotes, compared with the articles about the white women, which detailed their hobbies and idiosyncrasies, such as Alicia Ross's love of Led Zeppelin. Even today, I find it hard to imagine a newspaper article about a missing or murdered Indigenous woman that recounts her love of Led Zeppelin.

Whereas articles about the white women included large photographs, centrally placed, displaying the women as children or with family, the photographs of the Indigenous women were more documentary in nature: passport-sized, if included at all.

And the pronouns. The articles about the missing white women expressed fear about the predators stalking *our* streets, fracturing *our* communities, harming *our* daughters. In the articles about the Indigenous women, the pronouns were *they*: *Their* daughters. *Their* grief.

In the words of American crime writer James Ellroy: "Dead

people belong to the live people who claim them most obsessively." Of course, it helps if they have a platform to do so in public.

PBS anchor Gwen Ifill coined the phrase "missing white woman syndrome" (MWWS) in 2004, one year before *Washington Post* columnist Eugene Robinson published his satirical article on modern-day damsels. The media had begun to acknowledge its frenzy around white women who go missing and the comparable invisibility of violence against people of colour. "It's the meta-narrative of something seen as precious and delicate being snatched away," Robinson's article continues, "defiled, destroyed by evil forces that lurk in the shadows, just outside the bedroom window. It's whiteness under siege."[10]

In some ways, it's a problem of narrative laziness. White people dominate literature, art, and popular culture in the West because we are seen as universal beings. Similarly, missing or murdered white women and girls dominate the news because they are universal victims. See the damsel roped to railway tracks. See the woman in *King Kong*, whose name you probably don't remember even if you can picture her dangling from the gorilla's leathery hand. (Her name is Ann.) See Andromeda, nude and chained to the rocks. We do not tie men to railway tracks. If a man is chained to railway tracks, he probably did it himself. He will not be nude, and he will not await a princess to save him. Men are largely absent from "missing" narratives in the news—unless they're famous or rich, and absconding.

The moment we perceive ourselves as "rescuing a victim"— rather than preventing violence or protecting citizens—we stop respecting their agency as adults. In fact, the language we use to describe adults—non-damsel adjectives like *strong, independent,* or *self-sufficient*—gains a double edge. In a system where we rescue the universal victim, words like *strong* and *independent* also say "invulnerable." They say, "this person doesn't really need our help." We generally reserve such descriptors for people who aren't men, because in a patriarchy, we assume men are already strong, already independent, already self-sufficient. Like "strong women," they do not fit our picture of the ones who need protection, not in the same way. Krystal herself didn't fit the stereotype of a universal victim, and I wonder if that contributed to the system's inertia when she reported Bax's threats.

The damsel rhetoric around missing and murdered white women is objectifying and dehumanizing in its own right. When eighteen-year-old Natalee Holloway went missing on a class trip to Aruba, the *Los Angeles Times* described her, on the last night she was seen, as "an already inebriated blond" grasping a "sunset-colored rum drink." Waiters tossed a "serape over her bare shoulders" and poured "a stream of golden liquid into a mouth turned up like a baby bird's." The article moves on to describe the "pretty blond teenager . . . supine on the bar as a boy slurped Jell-O shots from her navel."[11] Hardly a dignified resting pose.

The journalist's language—"inebriated," "bare-shouldered," "supine," mouth "like a baby bird's," "slurped Jell-O shots from her navel"—further sexualizes, infantilizes, and otherwise demeans Holloway's body. The stories that rhapsodize on a woman's innocence or angelic status are equally disturbing, reducing female victims into a hackneyed virgin/whore binary.

The academic and media discourse around MWWS has problems too, often satirizing the seen victim into a "princess," as in Robinson's *Washington Post* article. The word *damsel* signifies an unmarried woman, with the connotation of someone who is not particularly strong, independent, or intelligent. The ridicule of dead women who *do* receive attention is another mode of victim-blaming.

Zach Sommers, who has studied the phenomenon of MWWS in the United States, notes a "two-stage filtration process" in the media, which disproportionately highlights the experiences of white people, and especially white women victims, suggesting they matter more, or they're more at risk. At the very least, Sommers concludes, these disparities imply news organizations will care more about, or more readily identify with, white victims.[12]

The ramifications of this are immense. Thousands of Indigenous women and girls have been murdered because their lives have been overlooked by government, police, and the media, or their lives have been framed as disposable, threatening, or not needing, or worthy of, protection. After death, their murders rarely attract the same urgency or panic in the news. I tried looking into other homicides in 1992, when Krystal Senyk was murdered, and while I found numbers, I struggled to find the victims' names. Partly, the problem is timing: 1992 preceded broad use of the internet and online news sources, so fewer articles have been archived online. The earliest available Statistics Canada report on national homicides, published in 1996, states that, between 1985 and 1994, on average two murders occurred per year in the Yukon, but the numbers don't get more specific.[13]

When I looked into this period further, I learned about twenty-one-year old Tina Washpan (known by her adoptive parents as Cindy Burk), who was murdered in 1990 while hitchhiking from Carmacks, Yukon, to Saskatchewan.[14] Her name appeared in the search returns only because her murderer was found and convicted sixteen years later. Tina's sister Diane Lilley shared their story during the Whitehorse hearings of the national inquiry. When Diane and her sisters were young, social services forcibly removed the children from their mother's home. First, the children tried to escape into the nearby woods, but the child welfare officials heard Tina, who was a baby, crying. Diane and two of her sisters would be sent to a residential school in Whitehorse, while Tina was adopted by a family in Regina. Their mother, Dorothy Washpan, had understood that if she stopped drinking, her children would be returned to her. She did so within the year, but her children were never permitted to come back. Diane realized later that, as a non-English speaker, their mother hadn't understood what the welfare officials had said. After their time at the residential school, Diane and her sisters were shuffled between foster homes. Meanwhile, in Saskatchewan, Tina was sexually abused by her adoptive father. Eventually, as young adults, Diane and Tina found their way back to their birth mother in Carmacks. Over the months they spent together, the sisters rediscovered their closeness, but Tina would soon leave Carmacks again—in part to remove herself from an abusive relationship. Tina regularly called her mother and sister as she made her way back south—so they worried when she didn't phone for two weeks. When they notified police, RCMP told them that "Tina's lifestyle meant she could be anywhere." In other words: she got herself into this mess; she doesn't really deserve our help; it's not worth our energy to find her.[15]

"She was taught to survive by hooking," Diane Lilley told the *Whitehorse Star* in 2017. "She was taught that by her adoptive dad."[16]

They didn't hear anything further from the RCMP until six months later, when Tina's remains were found off the Old Alaska Highway near Dawson Creek.

I don't know how police would have reacted if Tina were white, or otherwise employed, but I suspect their response wouldn't have been hostile indifference. And you can bet her name would have surfaced in the news before the RCMP arrested her killer in 2006.

No media outlets pitched Krystal as a princess or ingenue (though one early article described her as a "beautiful woman with a winning smile"). Krystal was a woman who compared her abdominal six-pack with men at the bar. She didn't need rescuing; she needed law enforcement to take her fears seriously. Maybe because Krystal didn't match the "universal victim" stereotype, the media was more concerned with the manhunt than eulogizing her. Locals were unnerved that an armed, violent, rageful man was on the loose, especially as sixteen residents of Whitehorse and Carcross were taken into protective custody. In early 1992, the population of the entire territory was under 28,000; 250 people lived in Carcross and 18,000 in Whitehorse. Fear travels fast in communities of this size. As a young white woman who worked for the government, Krystal met some of the criteria Sommers, Gilchrist, and others have outlined as constituting an identifiable and "valuable" victim. In short, her murder inspired first-person pronouns: *Our* community. *Our* safety. *Our* streets. However, I do wonder if her independence or physical strength made others assume she could take care of herself. Which she could. As many of us can. Until an enraged, armed individual wants us dead.

The Crown charged Ronald Bax with first-degree murder within two days of Krystal's death. Since then, three decades have passed. One of the factors the Crown must consider before it pursues prosecution is the complexity and length of the investigation, which could compromise the availability and credibility of witnesses, as well as the other evidence gathered. This process would only become more messy and expensive if prosecution required extradition from other countries, such as the United States. Whether formally or informally, police prioritize cases based on the likelihood of sending suspects to trial. Between more recent cases where the persons of interest remain in the area, and a thirty-year-old case where the lead suspect has vanished—and may indeed be dead—it would be in the public's interest to pursue, more rigorously, the former.

"As each new homicide comes in, that's the priority," said Whitehorse RCMP Superintendent Brian Jones in 2017. "They're all important, but they all can't be the priority on any given day. The historical cases we're working on, they suffer."[17]

To address this gap, the Yukon government provided the RCMP with $442,000 per year for three years, starting in 2018, to establish the Historical Case Unit. At the time this funding was announced, thirty-five homicides had been reported since 2000, and twelve remained unsolved.[18]

Thus we arrive at the paradox that lurks at the belly of this book: If Ronald Bax is alive, I want him caught. Yet I can't argue that the RCMP allocate further resources to catch him. Already, his manhunt attracted more money and attention than many historic cases in the Yukon combined. Surely, it helped that Krystal was a young woman who inspired first-person pronouns—even if that wasn't enough to keep her alive. I won't try to reconcile this paradox. However, I do think it's crucial to understand how all of this violence feeds itself. Who we see, who we believe, and who we help determines who stays safe.

April 13 / 97

To my Beautiful Daughter,

On April 13 / 97 will be 35 years old—5 years have gone so quickly. I am still working with RCMP. Uncle P—, Aunt S—, Aunt T—, my mother, Bill, our cousins talk about you all the time. A day does not go by Krystal that I do not think about you. Without memories there would be very little in life. So on this day of your birthday I am hoping you will have a good day with my Dad, Aunt M—, Bobby, Uncle M—, Grandpa E—, and all our family that is gone and friends.

Love always,

Dad xxxx

ooooo

xxxxxxxxx

16.

INVENTORIES

"I'm wearing a black jacket and I have a purposeful walk," Trish Colbert informed us over the phone as Myles and I waited in a Hamilton shopping mall. We were driving from St. Catharines back to Toronto in December 2019, two weeks after my trip to Mississippi. Trish had gone to school with Krystal. Krystal's brother Gord thought she might be able to share a few memories, so he'd passed along her number.

Trish arrived as described—in a black jacket and purposeful—and guided us toward the Jackson Square Food Court, recounting in a breath that she had been homeless but now lived across the street with her chihuahuas Hughie and Odin. I liked her instantly. She possessed a speed and frankness that I recognized, or felt comfortable mirroring. When I asked what coffee she wanted, she requested a four-by-four. I had to ask Myles, when she turned to greet a friend, what she meant. "Four creams, four sugars," he informed me, which I might have deduced, though I felt estranged from such Canadianisms, having grown up on the West Coast during the heyday of Starbucks.

Trish had lived next to Krystal and Gord in a town called North Pelham. Krystal had been two grades ahead of Trish: one of the older kids who sat at the back of the bus. Trish was small for her age, and other students bullied her, but Krystal would go out of her way to talk to Trish when no one else did.

"She was my saviour," Trish recalled. "My guardian." She described Krystal's calm—how she treated everyone with equal kindness. "She had such a big heart," she said. "It got her killed in the end, but she had such a big heart."

In her mid-twenties, Krystal moved to the Yukon and bought a property in Carcross from a man named Rabbit John. She devoted the next years of her life to rebuilding the cabin, hauling out seventeen truckloads of dirt, rabbit feces, and garbage. She had help— she'd call her brother, who had moved to the Yukon as well, and say, "You want to come for supper? Be there for nine a.m."—but she did an impressive amount herself. She built her own kitchen, sun porch, and greenhouse. She made the water run. One weekend, Gord stayed over, and they slept in sleeping bags on the floor. It was so cold in the morning, they could see their breath. They argued about who should get up to light the fire, both of them rattling in their sleeping bags. It became a competition to see who could hold their pee the longest.

When Krystal needed money to replace her cabin windows, she signed up for the Yukon Sourdough Rendezvous Festival, which included a spectacle of winter labours, such as axe throwing, dogsledding, chainsaw chucking, and flour packing. The reward for the flour-packing contest would pay for her windows. With minimal preparation, Krystal heaved 580 pounds of flour onto her back and schlepped the eleven metre course. She won. This after winning two other competitions that day, for left and right arm wrestling.

"Each new load of flour seemed to take every bit of Senyk's energy as she stared with intense concentration past the finish line, 11 metres away, and plodded forward," the *Whitehorse Star* reported in 1989.[1] After winning this round, Krystal tried to break a record by lugging 625 pounds, but she collapsed halfway through the course. "I could feel my knee tingle at 581 pounds and it was too tender on my knee, so I let go," Krystal later explained. Neither she nor her opponent were weight trainers. Krystal told the *Whitehorse Star* that her training came from building her house. "As a matter of fact, I'm going home now to put my sun windows in."

The year after that Rendezvous Festival, Krystal won two titles at the Canadian Armwrestling Federation competition in Winnipeg, which made her eligible for the world championship in Houston. "Looking back now, yes, I'm surprised I won," Krystal told the *Star* in 1990. "But I went in with a mindset that I was going to do my very best."[2]

Krystal goes on to describe her training strategy for the Houston contest, where her competitors would be using "a lot more technique." She practised Tai Chi and wanted to incorporate some of those principles into her training. In the end, she placed fourth in her weight class.

In a clip from that competition, the announcer introduces Krystal as "Canada, 4609." The crowd cheers, and Krystal waves her arm. She's wearing black track pants with thick white stripes down the sides, a polo shirt, and a red armband. She has glasses on and her hair is tied back. She wins the first round handily, but the next one appears effortful. You can see the strain on Krystal's face. Their arms are locked, trembling back and forth. Someone shouts, "Come on, Canada!" When she loses, she releases both arms in a flash of disappointment, or kicking herself.

"You're in, you're in, you're in!" someone shouts in the next round. Krystal grits her jaw in concentration. She's pressing her opponent's arm closer and closer to the table—then she does it, forcing her opponent's fist to the tabletop. The moment she realizes she's won, she slams her fist on the table in triumph, then immediately reaches for her opponent's shoulder, as if to say, "Good match."

She was "a little stressed," she said, about placing fourth in those championships, but it was the first time she had run into such serious competition. "Actually, it's the first time I've lost," she told a reporter the next morning. "One of my Canadian teammates asked how I was going to counter their 'back pressure and top roll' move,' and I said, 'what's that?'"[3] In the days before the championship, she prepared simply by "cutting a couple more cords of wood."

In addition to her athletic and physical activities, Krystal adored music. She and Gord would listen to cassettes as they cooked— everything from Barbra Streisand to Bowie to Meat Loaf. Gord recalls: "She wasn't someone you could place into one category . . . she could put on a cowboy shirt and a pair of jeans with a buckle, or a carpenter's belt, or go into an office dressed up, or put on a dress, stand on stage, and sing a song."

She played mandolin, banjo, and guitar. Their mother, Vera, sang in a band, Alberta Sunshine, for many years. When Krystal visited, she'd hop onstage with her. There's a mythic quality to how Gord describes their sound, how one voice would seep into the other. "It was unbelievably beautiful. They could harmonize so well. They would take turns doing the harmonies and you couldn't tell who was who. You would just see their mouths moving."

It's hard to approach Krystal without writing elegiacally. The problem with elegies is they only present someone in their absence, a presentation they can't control, an idealized view of them that functions mostly to console the bereaved. As someone who has grieved, and written of grief, I consider consolation a worthy pursuit. But elegies risk reducing a person's incalculability to abbreviation and refinement, the way you clean a body before burial and dress them up. Clothes you might recognize them in, down the line.

Krystal was buried in a long red skirt with a Ukrainian blouse tucked into the waistband, her expensive cowboy boots, a diamond stud in each ear. I know this because her cousin Jay saw her once, after death, leaning against a doorway. When he told Philip and Philip's wife at the time about this vision, they were stunned. They had dressed Krystal before the funeral. They were the only ones who knew what she was wearing.

Elegy mirrors the ritual of mourning—from grief to memory to self-soothing. It is hewn by longing, nostalgia, an impulse to preserve and adorn. It lacks the candour of a person who can tell you you got it wrong.

In the two pages her colleagues retrieved from a work computer, Krystal wrote:

```
The beginning is unremembered, its experi-
ences are untold, its presence is undeni-
able. That is not to say i do not belong
here, i do. I am here. The point is, I am
more than this time experience could allow:
I am different, I am special, I am more.
```

====

"It's probably better if you ask me more specific questions," said Mark Molnar, Krystal's best friend in Ontario, over the phone. "I don't like generalizing, in general."

"It's hard for me to remember specifics," he said eighteen minutes later. "I just remember that era."

The memories Mark offered match what other friends have told me: that Krystal was "always present, in the present moment." "What you see is what you get." "You always knew exactly where you stood with her."

His specifics—cruising in Krystal's Camaro through Niagara Falls, playing cards, talking about everything—belong to a past communicable now only through generalized time. I recognize his tone from when I travel and return home and a friend asks, "How was your trip?" I feel, for the moment, exhaustion, an inability to communicate anything meaningful without dulling my experience. "Good," I say, and move on.

If it's elegiac to write of Krystal now, it's also a labour of bricolage: to recover a person from the marks and material she left behind. Our obstacle is Krystal's absence: the years she never lived, her inability to speak for herself, to inscribe her own story. Our material is a necessary hodgepodge—scraps of paper, her father's notebooks, photos, home videos, condolences, memories—impressions at least thirty years old. The bricoleur makes do with whatever is at hand, writes Claude Lévi-Strauss: "a set of tools and materials which is always finite and is also heterogeneous because what it contains bears no relation to the current project."[4]

That is: Krystal did not write two pages of enigmatic stream of consciousness so that we might capture some snag of her. She did not buy cowboy boots, or a hunting knife, or a singing bowl so that we might glimpse her, indirectly, through the window of her inventory. Krystal did not give a mixtape to my neighbour Lynne so that thirty years later I might listen to it on repeat in an effort to hear, absorb, move, project-in-sound an instant (or eighty-eight minutes, on two sides), an echo of her interiority. The pages, the cowboy boots, the hunting knife, the singing bowl, the mixtape: when first procured, or created, over thirty years ago, they bore no relation to our current project of assembling them. Yet they're all we have.

"Both the scientist and 'bricoleur' might therefore be said to be constantly on the lookout for 'messages,'" says Lévi-Strauss. "Those which the 'bricoleur' collects are, however, ones which have to some extent been transmitted in advance."[5]

From Mark Molnar:

Krystal was my best friend. Colleen was Krystal's best friend. We were basically in each other's back pockets until I left for the Navy. Just before I left we had been having an argument or disagreement. I came back a year and a half later, and she met me at the train station. We picked up the same argument right where we left off.

We didn't have to see each other all the time. We just knew. Basically for a while there we always knew what each other was thinking.

That summer, I was supposed to go out there. We had made arrangements. I was at Brock at that point myself. I had gotten out of the Navy. I was going to Brock and I was taking theatre. And I was going out to work in one of the shows out there in Whitehorse. Then I got the news. I was going to go out and stay with her.

From Jay Senyk, Krystal's cousin:

We were very close. She was like a sister.
She had a '70s Camaro that she parked at our house
I used to sit in it and pretend to drive
It smelled like her
Once, I found a gold ring in the dash
I gave it back to her on a visit but she told me to hold on to it for her and keep it safe.

From Kari Wills, Krystal's stepsister:

She loved music.
Loved to write, especially letters.
She would spend hours on the phone with her dad, Philip.
She played guitar.

She was so independent.

She built her cabin herself.

An engineer, a hunter, yet at home in a pink skirt.

From Kim Hudson, colleague and friend:

Krystal was always present in the moment. Alive and open. Unafraid of life.

She hosted gatherings at her house: guitar, singing.

Everyone was welcome.

She taught herself to build. To paint.

She was extremely hardworking.

There was a light, a goodness about her.

She would be childlike in her joy.

She was fearless.

We would go out on Krystal's boat. I would paddle. Krystal would read me poetry.

She made sure everyone knew how she felt about them.

She left us all whole.

From Vera Campbell, Krystal's mother:

When she was young, we would sing together.

Music was a big part of our life.

She would go on hikes with the kids [Colleen's kids but also children from the Carcross/Tagish First Nation, where she lived].

Round them up and make some kind of show.

A smile on her face all the time.

She played guitar. She played better than I do.

I'm sitting here in my kitchen and I got my 6 string and my 12 string. I look at it every day and I try. But I can't control my feelings.

In Krystal's words:
```
Willingly, i choose to seek out the mis-
placed, searching for all that i was and am
currently able.
```

===

After Krystal died, her dad made a list of her belongings and how they would be divided.

Items for Phil:
Goose-down comforter
VCR tapes
Two rifles (police got it)
Tripod and cameras
Transit
Table + stool in sunroom
Rose wine glasses
Half C.D. Tapes
Kenwood cassette
Box speakers
Small pewter with stones
Easel
Half of negatives
1 arm-wrestling trophy
Flour-packing plaque
Wooden mule
Hunting knife (Paul's)
Binoculars
Bandanas
Canoe
Coffee container
Sleeping bag

Items for Colleen:
    Green vase
    Tall glove
    Rocker

Items for Vera:
    Leather belt and buckle
    Watercolour pencils
    Stones and crystals
    Bed
    Dresser
    All bedding
    All clothing and all footwear
    Chesterfield
    TV converter
    Kitchen table and 4 chairs
    Kitchen pots
    Towels, plates + knives
    Cutler mugs, glasses
    Pottery McPherson
    Pitcher + bowl on shelf
    Hand mixer
    Vonier Paul Game
    Fridge
    Stove
    Freezer
    Tools
    Hardwood
    Fish equipment
    Lazy boy chair
    New floor lamp
    All trophies except one

All outdoor clothing
Winter boots
All footwear
All books
Half arts
Half photos
All commercial cassettes
Half CDs
CD player
Receiver amp
Pitcher bowl
Banjo
Chet Atkins guitar
Gibson guitar
Galvanized tub
Lawnmower
Table saw
BBQ
Snowmobile
Hyundai car
Truck
Truck canopy
Computer printer
Mukluks
Fur mitts
Fishing tackle
Brand new wood stove in sunroom
Woodstove in cellar
Washer + dryer downstairs

INVENTORIES

The traces I carry of Krystal, passed from my neighbour Lynne
and Krystal's cousin Jay:

    2 pages from Krystal's work computer
    1 Nefertiti incense holder + incense sticks (Philip's)
    40 scanned photographs
    7 business cards
    2 roses, pressed between the pages of a 1991
NorthwesTel phone book
    1 mixtape:

Sweet Georgia Brown	*I Got a Name*
Take the A Train	*Comin' Around Again*
Walkin' My Baby Back Home	*You Belong to Me*
You Took Advantage of Me	*Only Have Eyes for You*
As Time Goes By	*Dream a Little Dream of Me*
One Less Set of Footsteps	*When I Sing*
If Wishes Were Changes	*Fallin' in Love Again*
Am I Blue	*Master of the House*
Under the Sycamore Tree	*Storms*
Mosaïque	*That's the Way the World . . .*
Atlanta June	*Only You*
El Verano	*Hurt*
Volare	*I'll Have to Say I Love You . . .*

Logically, its no wonder some members of the
human race find me unsettling. That is to
say, they cannot explain me. They are intimidated and choose to strike . . . Like the
flower in the weed, the beauty in the beast,
this earthly presence is both my captor and
my freedom. I am graced.

April 13 1999

To my Beautiful Daughter Krystal,

Another birthday has come and gone, but still no Bax to be found. Krystal up to date I have gone through 3 RCMP officers on your case and on the 4th one. After a time they all get transferred and you start anew again. 7 years, the time goes fast. But Krystal, memories last and last. But I do not forget about the past. I think of you every day, you are on my mind. 7 years the time goes fast. I am hoping one day justice will come at last. But the way our justice system works, who knows? Uncle F—, Aunt M—, Uncle B—, Mr. M—, Tom P—, all people you know, my dad, people that will take care of you should you need them.

Love always,

Dad

ooooo

xxxx

xxooo

17.

GORD

"It's like there's a calm lake. Then someone throws a rock into that lake. The ripples keep going and going, touching everything."

We're on Gord's deck, in Ponoka, Alberta. Me, Myles, Gord's partner Bridgette, and his childhood best friend Cordell. Gord's just left the table after seeing a photo of his sister he'd never encountered before—one of her holding a camera on the side of a road, grinning effulgently. Now he's smoking on the lawn, a few feet away.

When he returns to the table, he looks at me. "Can you send me that photo?"

"Of course."

After six years trying to understand Krystal's story, this is our last meeting with her family. The pandemic derailed earlier plans to visit, but as we sit together, it feels right to speak with Gord at this later stage. I feel better equipped to answer his questions about what we've been working on.

Bridgette prepared an incredible spread of food, accommodating every dietary restriction or preference: roast vegetable sandwiches for her and me, the vegetarians, the same with meat in them for Myles and Gord, a gluten-free wrap for Cordell. They'd packed their Harley-Davidson cooler with bottles and cans—hard iced tea, Red Stripe, ginger ale, soda water. We sat together all day, from noon until nine or ten, talking, listening, crying, our conversation studded with hockey banter and rounds of ladder ball. It was an hour or two before we realized that Gord had asked his best friend to be there for our visit—to drive in from British Columbia.

"What are friends for," Cordell had shrugged. He had ear-length hair, a reddish tan, a tattoo of a knuckle-duster on his arm. An oil guy turned convenience store owner turned ad hoc sailor. They'd trotted around together since Gord and his mom moved to Alberta when he was eight years old. Gord is more inked than his friend: a sleeve up his left arm. The tattoo looks like a creature of sorts, with tiers of gnashing teeth. He has the same cleansing blue eyes as his sister. He works with Bridgette, gutting homes that have been trashed or deteriorated and redoing them from the inside out. Gord's just returned from a big job in Fort McMurray—a luxury mansion with a bowling alley inside, destroyed by its hard-partying tenants.

"Bridgette's one of the best tapers and mudders in central Alberta," Gord says proudly. Until the Fort McMurray job, where he went solo while Bridgette stayed home to paint their own house, they hadn't spent a day apart in five or six years.

Bridgette is from BC originally. Her family had a go-kart track when she was growing up, and the two of them joke about how it still informs her driving. They tell us about the West Edmonton Mall go-kart track, which ascends three levels—how Gord couldn't keep up with her. She's also the one who asks the difficult questions about what Myles and I are working on: what the book will include, what our angle is. The last thing they want is for this to be a salacious thriller, glorifying Bax as the murderer. But they want the book out there. They want gender-based violence to be something people talk about bluntly, in the wide-open.

Gord's upbringing was different from Krystal's. After his dad left, he moved to Alberta with their mother, while Krystal stayed in Ontario with her dad's side of the family. Nestled between Calgary and Edmonton, Red Deer is a centre for oil and agricultural production. Or as Gord worded it, you're either a cowboy or an oilman (a loose reference also to Alberta's rival hockey teams). It's a town where you made your own fun as a kid, such as by driving as fast as you could, drunk, down "roller coaster road," or speeding at night without headlights till self-preservation instincts kicked in. It's a town where families swivelled from rags to riches and back to rags again. Where the cowboys or oilmen ran the local bars, to the point where if cops came in searching for someone, everyone in the place chucked their ashtrays at them until they hightailed it out of there. Where the more you talked about your family life as a kid, the more you realized that alcoholism, substance use, intimate partner violence, and absentee parents were devastatingly normal.

Like his friends, Gord started to party young. He was eleven when Krystal flew out one time to visit him and their mom. When she learned he was drinking, she said, "Oh you think you're so tough?" and challenged him to a contest. They sat across from each other at a table, both with forties of vodka. Gord asked to start with a few beers first—even at eleven, he was used to "warming up." So he went through three or four cans as Krystal sipped her forty. She'd drained two-thirds of it, while he'd quaffed less than half that, when he excused himself to vomit. "That's all?" she taunted. She was still calm and clear-eyed.

Years later, she confessed to him that her bottle had been filled with water. She'd wanted to teach him a lesson—to make him sick drinking so he wouldn't do it again. As a long-term strategy, it didn't have the desired effect, but Gord didn't have a lot of support to redirect him. The next year, Vera would move in with a well-to-do boyfriend. The caveat was he didn't like children, so

Gord wasn't invited into the arrangement. He was twelve when he dropped out of school and started working. His friends' parents would invite him for a meal, maybe help with his laundry or offer a place to shower. But for a while, he fended for himself.

Gord and Vera reunited when he was a teenager. He remembers a rare trip they all took to Hawaii when he was sixteen, Krystal in her early twenties. Krystal was too nervous to enter the water the first few days. *Jaws* had come out a decade earlier, when she was thirteen, and the film still terrified her. "There were a couple days where she was too scared to even use the toilet," Gord laughed, remembering.

He went snorkelling on that trip, and he wanted Krystal to see it all too—the vivid blooms of coral, the citrus-scaled fish, the abundance of luminous, slippery colour. Her love of nature must have gotten the better of her, because she went in with him the next day. However, the tide had shifted in such a way that the water went murky—no longer the turquoise lucidity he'd experienced the day before. She was feeling underwhelmed and ill at ease when something grazed her arm. That's all it took for her to get out of there, flailing onto the beach.

"You know how people say they don't care what others think? Krystal *really* didn't care," Gord tells us. Before she was hired as an engineer for the land claims department, Krystal worked for the City of Whitehorse. In one job, she was overseeing road construction on Two Mile Hill. Everyone else on the site was a man. If their work didn't meet industry standards, she told them to redo it—that was her responsibility. When they offered to buy her a drink instead, she said, "I don't want a drink, I want your work to be decent. Try again." It didn't matter what woman-hating names they called her after that.

It's two in the afternoon when the wine comes out. We're look-ing at photo albums, with pictures from that Hawaii trip. In the trunk—Vera's old hope chest—there are stacks of yearbooks. This is how we learn that Krystal rowed.

"Krystal, Turtle, you're the greatest 5-seat I've ever met in my life (+ the only one) + a terrific friend. Hope to see you a lot in the summer!" says one comment, from a fellow rower (who also calls herself Turtle).

"Krystal-Baby!! Best of luck to our most valuable oarswoman!"

Many notes congratulate her on the "well-deserved gold medal." Others offer some iteration of "I can't believe you wore a dress."

("Mom must have wrestled her into that one," Gord adds.)

Another note reads: "Dear Krys: to the wildest girl in school and the most conservative when in a bowling alley."

"Rocky, yes I know you starred in that movie, and you're the best bronco rider I've ever known," writes another friend.

One note feels especially poignant, amidst all the banter and in-jokes: "Krystal, how can I repay you? You saved my life in Charlene's bathroom. It was worth it. I got to know you better."

Even in high school, she was a woman known for her kind-ness, her strength, her discipline. But that didn't mean she took herself too seriously.

"What would Krystal be without her bandana?" the self-writ-ten bio reads under her graduation portrait. "Another forehead in the crowd."

Andrea Doty (a.k.a. Turtle) was the coxswain of the rowing team, charged with steering the boat, calling the race plan, yelling through a megaphone to motivate the other rowers. Krystal urged her to holler, which was hard for her at first, but eventually she found her voice (then lost it again after so much shouting). The rowing team required tremendous dedication—five a.m. starts, on the water by six, one hell of a workout, then rushing home to get showered and changed for class, only to train again after school.

Andrea was a couple of years younger than Krystal, and the self-proclaimed pipsqueak of the team, but Krystal took her under her wing. Krystal was her protector, while Andrea felt like her Gilligan, or "little buddy." Andrea's dad called her Turtle because of her affection for the reptile, and Krystal liked the nickname so much she called Andrea that too. Eventually, Andrea used the same term of endearment for Krystal.

At the time, Andrea's family was the kind that ate dinner together every night, and Krystal often joined them. One night, she went over to their house when Andrea wasn't home. Krystal asked Andrea's mother if she could stay anyway. She explained how she missed her own mom, who'd moved to Alberta. They spent the whole evening together talking.

The rowers were known for their underage drinking, but Krystal tended to avoid alcohol. Once, Andrea got caught and her dad made her swear an oath to him. Their heavy eight crew had just won the Schoolboy regatta, and the celebration on Henley Island would be the biggest party of her life. Her dad made her promise that she wouldn't touch a drop of alcohol at the celebration. He said, "If you want me to have faith in you, you're going to give me your word, and I'll trust you."

Everyone around them was sucking back booze, and Andrea had many drinks slotted into her hand, but she didn't take a sip. Krystal stood by her and said, "You don't need that crap. They're making idiots of themselves. You gave your dad your word." They sat on top of Krystal's Camaro and watched their friends get blitzed.

Andrea perceived Krystal as different from everyone else— smarter, more mature. She wasn't a trend follower and didn't care what was cool. She had a country look: jeans, bandana, checkered shirt, pigtails.

They lost touch after high school, Andrea moving to Toronto, Krystal eventually heading to the Yukon. Then Andrea saw the clip on *Unsolved Mysteries*. She happened to have the TV on when her friend's face flashed across the screen. She started shaking, shouting "No!" at the television. She called her mother, and they cried together over the phone.

"She was one of these rare people that you could never forget. She made people feel special—she certainly did with me. She was an incredible human being. It breaks my heart."

In the months after the murder, Gord tried to stay in Krystal's cabin, but there was a point where he had to get out of there. At night, he would hear a furious banging, as if someone was shaking all the walls and windows. He imagined it was Bax, ghosting around the woods, shooting at the house to make them miserable. The banging got so bad, it freaked out his girlfriend at the time—she would be crying, pleading for it to stop. Gord would step outside to look around, but never found anything, not a track in the snow.

A few days before the murder, Ron had cornered Gord at the bar and said, "What do you think of your sister?" Gord had shrugged him off, said, "I don't know. She does her own thing. I wouldn't mess with her." To this day, he wishes he recognized that confrontation as a red flag—wishes he had done something more. But how could he have known? And how could it have helped?

After a couple of hours sifting through the yearbooks and photo albums, we decide to put them back in the hope chest. We can tell

Gord feels tense with them in sight—all those memories so close to the surface. Cordell pours more wine. We're still on the deck—the clouds threatening rain, but slugging on. The sun sinking.

"I just want to stop having nightmares," Gord says. "I want to fall asleep without—" His voice cracks. He looks away, pinning his gaze on the lawn.

"He goes to bed with headphones," Bridgette explains, after a sticky swell of silence. "He has to listen to Netflix to fall asleep."

My own heart seizes as I understand how raw his pain is. Trauma has a way of rooting, toughening its hold on you, even as it worms underground.

Gord shares another story with us before we leave that night. How he was walking his dog out in the woods, shortly after Krystal's murder. This huge eagle swooped across his path, then vanished. He tried to find it, to spot where the eagle landed, but his dog wouldn't follow him. His dog who tagged his heels wherever he went—it wouldn't budge. It started barking and whining.

Gord kept scanning the surrounding trees. He pitched stones at one, where he thought the eagle might be lurking. He wanted to see it again, to send it soaring out. Then he heard her voice. As clear as if she was standing right next to him.

"I'm okay," she said. "Just look after Mom."

18.

BEYOND WHAT'S VISIBLE

Susan Sontag wrote that "memory is, achingly, the only relation we can have with the dead."[1] We see it everywhere: in museums documenting genocide; Holocaust memorials; residential school memorials; antiracism marches, the names remembered through megaphones; plaques commemorating massacres; tombstones; memorialized Facebook pages; ghost bikes. In a traditional vigil, you deny yourself sleep. It's a special wakefulness, observed when a loved one has died, or on the eve of a sacred day. It involves a particular, devotional watching: a witnessing of that person, their life, and everyone who loved them. As this book draws to an end, I've been turning a question over: What does justice look like for Krystal Senyk? In a society where the criminal justice system perpetuates its own harm, or at best functions like an institutionalized game of Whac-A-Mole, it's hard to feel content with "simply" finding Ronald Bax. And yet, that's part of it. For Krystal's family and friends, that's an important part. On the matter of what justice looks like, I reached back out to some of Krystal's loved ones to see what they had to say.

Krystal's cousin, Jay Senyk:

OK I talked it over with Dad, and we have quite the opposite ideas and thoughts. My thoughts are Krystal will never get justice. Her life was taken away by a jealous person; she was taken away from us way too early. I would love to see Ron caught and put behind bars for life. He has been on the run from the law, I get that, but the long and short of it is, he's alive and she's gone. He's had years of hiding from the police but is still free, which I believe is still not fair to Krystal or our family. Before Phil died, he said many times it was a big regret that Ron was never caught, and it bothered him that Ron was free. It bothered me to see how Phil was sad and would sit there and think about Krystal, always saying he would give everything to hear her laugh one more time. Ron took everything away from us so I would like to see him get his freedom taken away.

When I asked Jay about Paul Senyk's thoughts, he said:

He would rather catch Bax and deal with him personally.

Krystal's brother, Gord:

As far as justice goes for my sister Krystal and our family, I truly believe "an eye for an eye" is the only true justice in an example of the lowest level of human behaviour, such as this. I was sickened, and my family is traumatized to this day. There is no recovery for a lifelong trauma like this. It changes a person's fundamental character traits to the core and never leaves you. How, after so much time has gone by, with this in my life, can any type of justice repair or replace the loss we suffered in our lives? There are a few to blame and many that suffer from this disaster which I believe should have been a completely avoidable tragedy. I'll always love you, Krys.

He ran these thoughts past Bridgette before he sent them to me. She offered, "So, an eye for an eye would be the justice you would have wanted, but after all this time there is no justice that can repair it." Gord included her response with his, adding, "That's what I was trying to get across. Exactly what B said."

Krystal's close friend Suzanne:

Justice to me would be Ron being found or turning himself in and going to prison for taking Krystal's life. He wasted not only her life but his own. He had a lot of potential too and had a good wife and two beautiful children. Too bad he didn't have a good childhood, and maybe that contributed to his anger issues, but it's still no excuse.

Krystal's friend and colleague Elizabeth Hanson:

I don't know if the justice is for Krystal, but for all the ones on her behalf who would like to see closure. Closure that says, here was a bright young woman, who was highly principled, hardworking . . . Nobody should lose their life. It's not vengeance, but there should be some accounting for that. I don't know if it is possible to actually provide justice for Krystal, but I do still believe that her death was a classic case, repeated too many times, where the woman is simply not believed. So, if we can achieve anything, I hope it is that when a woman expresses fear of harm, that she is not gaslighted, that she is taken seriously, and that she is supported in her right to being safe in her own home.

Since 2000, Barbara McInerney has served as the executive director of the transition home where Krystal and Colleen sought shelter on the last night of Krystal's life. When I asked McInerney what justice looked like for people experiencing gender-based violence, she said: "Most women? They just want it to stop. Most women I know, who are dealing with violence today, they don't want revenge. They don't even want him to go to jail. They want it to stop. They want to be free. It's very simple. And they want to feel as if they've got equality within the system."

What would equality within the system look like? I asked.

"That women are believed. That child protection in domestic violence cases—that the file is put in the man's name."

McInerney explained that the vast majority of child protection files are listed under the mother's name, which means the mother is the one penalized for her partner's abuse, for not providing a safe environment for her kids. "Equality within the system would mean women are always accompanied by police to pick up her items. That our sexual histories are not brought into sexualized violence cases within courts. That—God—that Crown lawyers don't use neutralizing language that the defence can then use to lessen a sentence or lose the case."

An example of neutralizing language, she said, might be *he kissed her*.

No, it was a rape. He forced his mouth onto hers and stuffed his tongue down her throat. Nothing consensual about it. The pedophile *groomed* the child . . .What are you doing when you're grooming? It's an affectionate term. That does not explain what that perpetrator did: to set up being able to rape a child. We use neutralizing terms all the time. It undermines the victims, it conceals the responsibility of offenders. But we don't like using language like *he forced his mouth on her*. A lot of times we don't talk like that. To our detriment. *Sex tourism*. Really? Children can't consent to sex, so why are we talking about it like sex? It's an organized rape of children.

It feels like I'm slapping people on the face when I talk that clearly, but by using neutralizing language, we are colluding with the offender, and we are concealing the level of violence. We're making it a relationship issue. It's not a relationship issue. It's not about anger management. It's about *strategic gender-based violence*.

In his Judgment of Inquiry, coroner Larry Campbell determined that it was reasonable for the RCMP to deny Krystal Senyk an escort home that night. That it would have been irresponsible to take her from a place of safety to a place of risk. That Krystal herself was strong-willed and independent, and she refused to be pushed around. If we accept these conclusions, then whose responsibility is it to resolve gender-based violence? Might her life have been saved if she was more demure? More docile? Is that what justice looks like?

To leverage Krystal's independence as a rationalization for why she got killed places the onus on the wrong person. Krystal was acting reasonably in wanting to go home after weeks away. She was acting reasonably in wanting to make sure her pipes weren't freezing, to feed her animals, to return the truck she borrowed from a friend. She was reasonable to refuse "living [her] life according to Ron," her last words to her friend Suzanne. And she was reasonable to fear him, to ask for help.

"I can understand police wanting to create safety and make their job easier," said McInerney. "I get that. But women are adults and have their right to agency, to have their decisions respected. It's about respecting women's choices and trying to keep that as safe as you possibly can."

If for Krystal's friends and family, justice also involves Ronald Bax's capture, the question left looming is: Where is he? Is he living somewhere as a fugitive, under the radar, or did he kill himself after Krystal's murder?

The forensic psychologists who studied the file in the mid-nineties suggest Bax was erratic and despondent enough to make suicide a real possibility. His body and firearm were never found, but as numerous locals have remarked, the Yukon is an easy place to disappear in. Dead or alive. Especially for someone as skilled as Ronald Bax.

The Yukon is also a mineral-rich territory and the site of many abandoned mines. According to Murray Lundberg, the writer behind the ExploreNorth Blog and author of *Fractured Veins & Broken Dreams*, a book about Yukon mines, there are mines everywhere in the Carcross area. While no one has ever created an inventory of the ones still accessible, there are at least fifty openings within two hours of Carcross, leading to at least twenty kilometres of underground tunnel. Some are short—you can shine your flashlight in and see the collapsed end of it. Others stretch far beyond what's visible.

If Bax didn't want to be found, a mine shaft would provide a covert resting place. There are more accommodating locations to end your life, surely, but perhaps comfort isn't a concern when you're so close to that call. The fact that he never tried to contact Colleen or his sons supports the suicide theory, wherever he might have done it, unless his will to start fresh somewhere else surpassed the love and possessiveness he felt for his family. Given he murdered his wife's best friend, that idea doesn't feel too farfetched either.

Some fugitives do disappear for decades. In January 2021, police in Barrie, Ontario, arrested a suspect in the 1994 murder of Katherine Janeiro. "The fact that today we can hold someone accountable for the violent death of Katherine Janeiro should serve as proof that no homicide case is ever closed until an arrest is made," stated Barrie Police Chief Kimberley Greenwood.[2] (At the time of writing, the accused has yet to be tried.)

Meanwhile, in 2019, an arrest was made for the 1973 murder of eleven-year-old Linda Ann O'Keefe. Police received a tip that eventually led them to collect a sample of her killer's DNA. The tip came several months after the Newport Beach Police Department live-tweeted Linda's story, from her perspective, on the last day of her life. Orange County District Attorney Todd Spitzer said the live tweets didn't necessarily lead to the identification of the perpetrator, but they "created an awareness and opened doors for us to have this case pursued with renewed effort."[3]

Closer to the time and place of Krystal's murder, an individual was captured in 1992 for murdering the Whitehorse man he'd lived with nineteen years earlier. Like Bax, the killer disappeared after the murder. He was arrested two decades later in Naples, Florida, for violating US immigration laws.[4]

I wonder what the police reports said in these historic cases about the probability of suicide. No doubt many disappeared murderers *have* ended their lives, somewhere discreet, where the body would be difficult to find. They're not in the media because a case unsolved twenty, thirty, or forty years later is not a news story. But how often do investigators theorize suicide simply because they don't have evidence to the contrary? Especially decades later, when the death of the perpetrator grows more and more likely. Even if Bax didn't kill himself in 1992, he could still be dead. A lot can happen in thirty years, especially if circumstances lead you to live a less than monastic lifestyle.

So what happened to Ronald Bax? Whether he's dead or alive, I hope one day we know the answer. As someone who's been turning stones over in this story for only six years, rather than thirty, I do still have some of that: hope.

After Krystal died, Gord and Vera wanted to finish the house for her. They worked with their friend Eddie, Krystal's neighbour, who'd always come over to help her with the construction. Together, they completed the sunroom, as well as a deck to surround the house. They constructed a two-storey, 960-square-foot addition—larger than the original cabin. After that, the work still didn't feel finished. They added a garage, now tripling the size of the first structure. Some of the neighbours raised their eyebrows— "Isn't it big enough yet?" The answer was no. Gord and Vera were building that house for Krystal, communing with her in some way, picking up the work she'd left half-finished, elaborating on it. Speaking to their daughter, their sister, through the work her hands had crafted, completing her sentences. No, it wasn't big enough yet.

How could it ever be?

Krystal Senyk
murdered on March 1,
1992 by Ronald Bax
in Carcross, YT

I am the collective gathering of all my experiences. My behaviours and beliefs have evolved throughout countless ages and have currently choosen to manifest themselves in the human form present on this earth, in this time. You see, i am part of a continuum. A linkages of lives each unique unto itself but forming a complete picture of the essense of the life it was and currently is. The beginning is unremembered, its experiences are untold, its presence is undeniable. That is not to say i do not belong here, i do. I am here. The point is, I am more than this time experience could allow: I am different, I am special, I am more. Logically, its no wonder some members of the human race find me unsettling. That is to say, they can not explain me. They are unsettled at the non-conformity of mental structure. They are intimidated and choose to strike in the most interesting fashions. They tease, they pry they become frustrated and angered when reactions expected are not received. I believe only they limit themselves as I believe I too have the potential to limit myself as well. Regardless, my earthly environment is truly enjoyable in its natural beauty. Like the flower in the weed, the beauty in the beast, this earthly presence is both my captor and my freedom. I am graced.

I am not unaware of the influential powers my unguarded energies harbour. Willingly, i choose to seek out the misplaced, searching for all that i was and am currently able. Periodically, i believe i summon what may be more than i am currently able to assimilate. In rousing these patterns of thought, i can be easily thrown from the societal positioning i find adventageous to incorporate. Delicately balanced i then choose to withdraw from the masses shielding myself in an armour of solitude until i have healed leaving me less vulnerable to queery and misunderstanding.

What is it that makes this moment different from the countless others when i have stood right here, towel in hand, drying my body preparing for the challenges of this, or any other day? Still wet from the bath, with water dripping from my skin, i am only aware of the need to sensitize. The cooling water heightens my sensory awareness and i am all at once charged with the strength of determination. Naked i stand, curious and tempted by my own reflection. When i choose to look, the mirror often reflects the face i am familiar with alas, the eyes become haunting in their depth. My hands reach for the rim of the sink for i will need support. Veins close to the skins surface from the heat of the bath increase the preception of power as my grip tenses the muscles of my upper body. Leaning intently forward i see a human, a picture of seemingly demanding physical presence. I am amazed and arrogant at once.

Looking deep within myself, i realize i am different which makes me both proud and comfortable. I see a spirit captured by the memories of previous existances entrapped in a human body starved for passion. Thinning with each passing year, this body is enticed with tempestuous samplings of fine dining portioned throughout a gathering of self inflated critics of an elite gourmet magazine. Undernourished, this

essence is reaching for vitality and recognition simeltaneously.
Through all of this i have yet to understand how but a mortal is to
effectively master immortal behaviour seemingly demanded of me, by me.

The request comes from a voice soothingly familiar to my core but
unknown from my aquaintances on this earth. With resonate
determination i search , absorbed within my line, until this face
becomes a sea of darkness and my world centres on the depth perception
of lives once lived but now fragmented in memory recall. Intently, i
stand looking for a glimmer of recognition and periodically it is mine.
Revelations of a most unusual nature occur and i am comfortable with
these. I see glimmers of light illuminating a shadowed corner of my
subconscience once thought lost to fear. It is the rememberance of
these experiences that lead me comfortably along my path of transition.
At times, my present face fades from site allowing a face lost to the
past to reappear where the recognizable once was presented.
Transformed from the conformation currently granted, my face
reconfigures itself to resemble that which i no longer am. I now stand
and see a face belonging to my essence. Perhaps now dispised, i am
confronted with this memory and it consciously becomes mine to react as
i may. This face that i was is there for me to look directly into. A
vivid reminder of the errors previously rendered and my inability to
overcome my shortcomings.

The deeper i look into the blue green, the further into the trance i am
pulled until i become so afraid i slap myself with the sensory
perception of the cooling air settling on my hardened nipples. All at
once i am shivering looking for clothing to cover a body that begs to
be uncovered. Skin, taunt with the musculature of youthfulness,
covered by cloth a lovers eyes could remove. I am trapped. I am
caught in a body unfit for assimilation into the vast majority of the
societal structure and the mental capacity not to find this acceptable.
The more i try to compromise, the more i do battle with myself, the
more i entrench my belief in myself. I am good and bad all at once.

yin and yang?, no, confused, no. determined would be a better
description. an outcast, answer yet unknown   if this is so, then it
will only be to some and then, so be it if it may.

As i reach for the towel that will dry the now shivering body, my hand
brushes the skin that it is to dry. responsive, this skin is new and
fresh. reaching out for a touch, most selective of the source my sense
rush to the surface and once again i am face to face with the truth of
my continuum.

ENDNOTES

CHAPTER 1

1   A pseudonym.

2   Maggie Nelson, *Jane: A Murder* (Berkeley: Soft Skull, 2005), 23.

CHAPTER 2

1   The following section supplements the details of the transition home's report with Suzanne's recollections of that night and the following day.

CHAPTER 3

1   Maggie Nelson, *The Red Parts: Autobiography of a Trial* (London: Vintage, 2015), 5.

2   Nelson, *The Red Parts*, 7.

3   Jacques Derrida, *Specters of Marx: The State of the Debt, the Work of Mourning and the New International*, trans. Peggy Kamuf (New York: Routledge, 1994), 217.

4   Derrida, *Specters of Marx*, 221.

5   Carl Jung, "Synchronicity: An Acausal Connectivity Principle," in *Collected Works of C.G. Jung*, vol. 8, trans. R.F.C. Hull (Princeton, NJ: Princeton University Press, 2011), para. 924.

6   Jung, "Synchronicity," para. 919.

7   Derrida, *Specters of Marx*, 220.

CHAPTER 5

1   Elizabeth Hanson, "Remember Krystal, Remember Them All," *Yukon News*, March 2, 2012.

2   Susan Treggiari, *Roman Social History* (New York: Routledge, 2002), 81.

3   Catharine MacKinnon, *Toward a Feminist Theory of the State* (Cambridge, MA: Harvard University Press, 1989), 190.

4   William Blackstone, *Commentaries on the Laws of England*, vol. 1

(Oxford: Clarendon Press, 1773), 430.

5   Anne Kingston, "We Are the Dead," *Maclean's*, September 17, 2019.

6   Kingston, "We Are the Dead."

7   "Murder Victim's Sister Wants Provocation Defence Eliminated," CBC News, May 19, 2000.

8   "Klassen Gets Five Years for Manslaughter," *Whitehorse Star*, December 2, 1996.

9   Brain R. Decker, "Violence and the Private: A Girardian Model of Domestic Violence in Society," *University of Pennsylvania Journal of Law and Social Change* 11 (2008): 105.

10 "Femicide Is Preventable," Canadian Femicide Observatory for Justice and Accountability, 2020.

11 Maire Sinha, "Section 3: Intimate Partner Violence," *Juristat* (Ottawa: Statistics Canada, 2013).

12 "Trends & Patterns in Femicide," Canadian Femicide Observatory for Justice and Accountability, 2020.

13 World Health Organization, "Devastatingly Pervasive: 1 in 3 Women Globally Experience Violence," news release, March 9, 2021.

14 Sandy James, Jody Herman, Susan Rankin, Mara Keisling, Lisa Mottet, and Ma'ayan Anafi, "Executive Summary," *Report of the 2015 U.S. Transgender Survey* (Washington, DC: National Center for Transgender Equality, 2016), 13.

15 Cherami Wichmann, "Male Survivors of Intimate Partner Violence: A Summary," *Victims of Crime Research Digest* 14 (Ottawa: Department of Justice, 2021).

16 Wolf-Dieter Narr, "Systemic Violence: Typicalities and Peculiarities of Violence in Our Time," *Humanitas* 1 (Spring 2002), 16.

17 Narr, "Systemic Violence," 17; italics added.

18 Sara Darling, "Women's Day Marked, Not Celebrated," *Yukon News*, March 11, 1992.

19 Darling, "Women's Day Marked."

20 This acceptance speech for the 1992 Wonderful Woman Award was sent to us directly by Helen Fallding.

21 Darling, "Women's Day Marked."

22 Lisa Tremblay, "Presentation to the Canadian Panel on Violence Against Women," Lesbian Issues Committee of the Yukon Status of Women Council (Whitehorse: April 1992.)

23 Tremblay, "Presentation."

24 Tremblay, "Presentation."

25 Tremblay, "Presentation."

26 Sherryl Yeager, "Abusive Men Use Senyk's Murder to Back Threats," *Whitehorse Star*, April 24, 1992.

27 Sherryl Yeager, "Man Jailed Three Months After Uttering Threats," *Whitehorse Star*, April 14, 1992.

CHAPTER 6

1 In the excerpts from Philip's journals, I have omitted full names to protect the privacy of individuals identified.

2 Caroline Murray, "Father Regrets That Murder Case Won't Be Aired," *Whitehorse Star*, March 22, 1995.

3 Sherryl Yeager, "Murder Victim Wasn't Refused Protection, Coroner Concludes," *Whitehorse Star*, June 24 1993.

4 Yeager, "Murder Victim."

5 Yeager, "Murder Victim."

6 Coroner Larry Campbell, "Judgment of Inquiry," June 23, 1993, Whitehorse, YT.

CHAPTER 7

1 Yvon Dandurand, *Firearms, Accidental Deaths, Suicides and Violent Crime: An Updated Review of the Literature with Special Reference to the Canadian Situation*, working document prepared for the Department of Justice Canada, September 1998.

2 Paul Chard, "Search Costs Hit $80,000," *Yukon News*, March 27, 1992.

3 "Bax Manhunt Is Cut Back," *Yukon News*, March 13, 1992.

4 Sherryl Yeager, "RCMP Had Sought Second Person in Senyk's Murder," *Whitehorse Star*, March 30, 1992.

CHAPTER 8

1 A pseudonym.

2 Rebekah M. Yearout, "Man wanted by Canadian police may be in county," *Press Register*, Friday March 13, 2015 (Clarksdale MS).

CHAPTER 9

1 To preserve their privacy, I have replaced the names of most individuals in Mississippi with pseudonyms.

2 The name of the store has been changed.

CHAPTER 14

1 A pseudonym.

CHAPTER 15

1 Payne Lindsey, "Cold as Alaska," August 7, 2016, in *Up and Vanished*, podcast, produced by Tenderfoot TV.

2   Sharon Butala, *The Girl in Saskatoon* (Toronto: HarperCollins, 2009), 1.

3   Pat Reavy, "Elizabeth Smart Among People's 'Most Beautiful,'" *Deseret News*, April 30, 2005.

4   John Berger, *Ways of Seeing* (London: BBC and Penguin Books, 1973), 45.

5   "Trends & Patterns," Canadian Femicide Observatory for Justice and Accountability, 2020.

6   "Homicide in Canada, 2020," *The Daily* (Ottawa: Statistics Canada, November 25, 2021), 5.

7   Ryan Flanagan, "Why Are Indigenous People in Canada So Much More Likely to Be Shot and Killed by Police," CTV News, June 19, 2020.

8   "Homicide in Canada, 2020," 5.

9   Kristen Gilchrist, "'Newsworthy' Victims?: Exploring Differences in Canadian Local Press Coverage of Missing/Murdered Aboriginal and White Women," *Feminist Media Studies* 10, no. 4 (2010): 6.

10   Eugene Robinson, "(White) Women We Love," *Washington Post*, June 10, 2005.

11   Carol J. Williams, "In Holloway Case, Aruba Also Suffers," *Los Angeles Times*, June 4, 2007.

12   Zach Sommers, "Missing White Woman Syndrome: An Empirical Analysis of Race and Gender Disparities in Online News Coverage of Missing Persons," *Journal of Criminal Law and Criminology* 106, no. 2 (2016): 311.

13   Orest Fedorowycz, "Homicide in Canada – 1996," *Juristat* (Ottawa: Statistics Canada, 1997), 13.

14   Sidney Cohen, "I Had to Be the Grown-Up One for My Two Sisters," *Whitehorse Star*, June 1, 2017.

15   Cohen, "I Had to Be the Grown-Up."

16   Cohen, "I Had to Be the Grown-Up."

17   Philippe Morin, "RCMP Workload in Yukon 'Not Sustainable,' Says Superintendent," CBC News, July 5, 2017.

18   "Yukon Gives RCMP More Money to Solve Homicide, Missing Persons Cases," CBC News, March 6, 2018.

CHAPTER 16

1   Rhoda Metcalfe, "Flour-Packing Was Endurance Test," *Whitehorse Star*, February 27, 1989.

2   Bernie Adilman, "Yukoner Wrestles Arm Titles," *Whitehorse Star*, September 24, 1990.

3   "Whitehorse Arm Wrestler Grabs Fourth-Place Finish at World Championships," *Whitehorse Star*, November 5, 1990.

4   Claude Lévi-Strauss, "The Science of the Concrete," in *The Savage Mind* (Chicago: University of Chicago Press, 1966), 17.

5   Lévi-Strauss, "The Science of the Concrete," 20.

CHAPTER 18

1   Susan Sontag, *Regarding the Pain of Others* (London: Penguin Random House, 2019), 101.

2   Kim Phillips, "Barrie, Ont., Police Make Arrest in 1994 Homicide of Katherine Janeiro," CTV News, January 14, 2021.

3   Amy Wang, "Police Revived a 1973 Murder Case by Live-Tweeting a Girl's Last Day. Now, a DNA Match Has Led to an Arrest," *Washington Post*, February 20, 2019.

4   Paul Chard, "Murder Suspect Nabbed in Florida," *Yukon News*, March 1992.

Eliza's

ACKNOWLEDGMENTS

Researching this case has been a labour of collective remembering. Above all, I am grateful for the trust of Krystal's family. Gord Campbell, Vera Campbell, Jay Senyk, and Paul Senyk: thank you for letting us into your lives. Thank you for sharing your memories, your keepsakes, your stories, and your heartache. This book is for you.

Thank you to everyone who took time to speak with Myles and me over the past several years: Chuck Bertrand, Trish Colbert, Suzanne Gignac, Elizabeth Hanson, Kim Hudson, Bob Kapala, Jean Kapala, Murray Lundberg, Barb McInerney, Claudia McPhee, Mark Molnar, Adam Morrison, Rick Noack, Eloise Spitzer, Kari Wills, and Bill Wray. For many of you, talking about Krystal has involved combing through painful memories and experiences. Thank you for your courage in sharing your truths.

Thank you to those who spoke to us anonymously, including many of the people I met in Mississippi. I am grateful for your time and openness.

This book would not exist if Lynne Partel had not dropped Krystal's pages on my doorstep one July day in 2015. Thank you for trusting me, as well as for sharing your own memories and reflections.

Thank you to the Whitehorse RCMP members who

cooperated where they could: Const. Julia Mahoney, Chief Supt. Scott Sheppard, and especially Const. Craig Thur, who has devoted years to resolving Krystal's murder. Despite your demanding workload, you continued to speak with Myles and me long after you were responsible for this case. I'm grateful for your time and your commitment to finding and sharing the truth.

I am indebted to everyone who read an early version of this manuscript and offered their feedback: Kathryn Cass, Dana Holtby, Anna Metcalf, Jacinta Mulders, Jesse Robertson, and Erin Robinsong. Thank you. I'm also grateful for the support of everyone willing to listen and talk out ideas as I pursued this story, including Leanne Dunic, Nathan Hamilton, Sandra Huber, Ilona Jurkonyte, Michael Nardone, and Kasia Van Schaik.

Thank you to my agent, Karolina Sutton, and to my editor, Nicole Winstanley, for championing this book when it was only a fledgling preoccupation. Thank you to everyone at Penguin Random House who has had a hand midwifing this book into being.

To the Writers' Trust of Canada and Access Copyright Foundation Marian Hebb Research Grants program: thank you for your material support, which meant everything while I was writing and researching this story.

I am endlessly grateful to the ones in my life who have supported this work directly and indirectly over the years: Angela, Iris, Meagan, Patrick, Rachel, Rose, Ryan—and Brigid.

Jasmine, thank you for always being ready, and with me. Thank you also to Kestrel, for your long-distance (yet no less mighty) support, and to Sandra. Your friendship means more than you all know.

Myles—you have been an irreplaceable collaborator from the beginning. Thank you for your hours at the archives, your interviews, your devotion to this project, your trust, and for our countless sounding-board sessions.

Thank you, Mom and Jesse, for giving me the foundations and guidance to follow my heart. And thank you, Arnaud, for your love, your listening, and your care.

Myles's
ACKNOWLEDGMENTS

Firstly, I would like to thank the Yukon Archives and its staff for helping me dig up a wealth of information from its impressive collection of newspaper archives on microfilm. A debt of gratitude is owed to Sherryl Yeager, a former *Whitehorse Star* reporter whose numerous articles I found there gave us a much better understanding of this tragedy and its aftermath.

I am grateful to everyone who took the time to speak to me about Krystal or Ron. Despite reliving traumatic memories, you chose to open up to me in an effort to help preserve Krystal's legacy: George Balmer, Marilyn Buchanan, Vera Campbell, Robin Charman, Trish Colbert, retired Niagara Regional Police detective Thomas (Tom) Daley, Andrea Doty, Jan Forde, Paul Gray, Liz Hanson, Kim Hudson, Helen Gartner, Suzanne Gignac, Sheri Lash, Bruce Martel, Roland McCaffrey, Barb McInerney, Claudia McPhee, Yohanna Quackenbush, Betty Sutton, Connie Thompson, Dianne Villeseche, and Paul Warner. Thank you for putting your trust in me, and in us.

Thank you to those who pointed me in the right direction, who shared a document or contact information for a source, or who were just helpful in general: Nadine Bell, Logan Braasch, Helen Fallding, Cheryl Cannell Lawrence, Murray Lundberg, Kate White, Bill Wray, and everyone else who took the time to contact me through my website.

I am grateful to Whitehorse RCMP Const. Craig Thur for his invaluable contributions since 2015. Craig has been involved in this case for well over a decade, in one way or another, and has always been generous with his time and input (despite this still being an open investigation). I would also like to thank other RCMP members, among them Const. Julia Mahoney, Coralee Reid, and Chief Supt. Scott Sheppard, for their assistance over the years.

Thank you to Nicole Winstanley for believing in us from the start and for your unwavering support. We really needed someone like you to understand the importance of this story, and you became its greatest champion.

Notable thanks to retired RCMP member Rick Noack for his incredibly helpful guidance and advice, for believing in us, and for providing valuable context when it comes to police investigations. Thank you to daughter Sarah Krause for helping us track Rick down.

Thank you to Jay Senyk, the Niagara region's #1 tour guide, who was instrumental in giving us access to documents belonging to his uncle (and Krystal's father) Phil. Thank you for welcoming us into your home and showing us around in 2019. Your kindness and generosity know no bounds.

Thank you to Linda Rapp for her positive influence on my life. We miss you dearly.

This book would not be possible without Gord Campbell's input. I can't imagine how painful it must be for you to relive these memories, but your support over the years has kept this project, and your sister's legacy, alive. Despite your allegiance to the Maple Leafs, I am indebted to you and can never find the words to thank you enough for your kindness and friendship. Thank you to Bridgette for your support and understanding.

Eliza, I am truly grateful for our serendipitous encounter in the summer of 2018. Thank you for your patience, optimism, and dedication, but especially for embracing my role of contributor and allowing me to participate in this book.

I would like to acknowledge the love and support I've received from my family since I started working on this project in 2015: France, Ken, and Sean, thank you for continuing to inspire and believe in me. I love you. Thank you to the O'Connor and MacDonald families for your generosity and hospitality, and for always making me laugh with your ridiculous antics.

My greatest appreciation is for my partner, Aimee, my constant source of motivation and inspiration. You take care of me and nurture me, and you gave me the support I needed to work on this. You never cease to amaze and impress me. I love you. Bobbi, you greatly improve my quality of life, and despite your incessant barking, I am thankful for your love and companionship.

ELIZA ROBERTSON's 2014 debut story collection, *Wallflowers*, was shortlisted for the East Anglia Book Award and selected as a *New York Times Editors' Choice*. Her critically acclaimed first novel, *Demi-Gods*, was a *Globe and Mail* and *National Post* book of the year and the winner of the 2018 QWF Paragraphe Hugh MacLennan Prize. She studied creative writing at the University of Victoria and the University of East Anglia, where she received the Man Booker Scholarship and Curtis Brown Prize. In addition to being shortlisted for the CBC Short Story Prize and Journey Prize, Eliza's stories have won the Commonwealth Short Story Prize, Elizabeth Jolley Prize, and 3Macs carte blanche Prize. She lives in Montreal.

MYLES DOLPHIN is a communications specialist and a former journalist in all three Canadian territories. Newspapers he has worked for include the *Hay River Hub*, *Nunavut News* and *Yukon News*. He currently lives in Victoria, B.C. with his wife Aimee and Pomeranian Bobbi. *I Got a Name* is his first book collaboration.